TRU

The Battle for America

"Injustice anywhere is a threat to justice everywhere."
Dr. Martin Luther King Jr.

Hanne Nabintu Herland

PAPER TRUE

TRUMP: The Battle for America by Hanne Nabintu Herland

Disclaimer: This book offers factual information and viewpoints that might be useful in arriving at an understanding of the events of our time. We believe that the information comes from reliable sources but cannot guarantee the information to be free of mistakes and incorrect interpretations.

Front Cover: Kristian Kapelrud.

Portrait Photo: Paul Bernhard.

ISBN: 978-1-8381277-7-0

eISBN: 978-1-8381277-6-3

This book is dedicated to the President of the United States, Donald Trump for his efforts to help America become great again

Content

Donald Trump, China and the Corona Scandal

CHAPTER 1

Trump and the Fight Against China and the Super-Rich

Donald Trump may be the most demonized President in US history, simply because his enemies own the media and the established globalist elite. With his "America First" slogan, he launched a massive attack on the globalist billionaire's empire that for decades has benefitted from the outsourcing to jobs and wealth to Communist China and the ultra-rich.

Over 90 % of the US media is owned by only 6 corporations with widespread interest in the development of a globalist, transnational capitalist system that profits from lack of national sovereignty.[i] The globalist business model is dependent on weak nation states, that easily may be overrun by global corporations that crush the middle class and local businesses.

And globalism has worked, it has reinforced an international economic model that departs from the nation-based capitalist system and benefits the ultra-rich in an unprecedented scale.

Globalism has produced a system in which around 50 individuals now own over 50 % of world assets,[ii] only made possible by the transnational business model that refuses to redistribute wealth when outsourcing jobs to China and other cheap labor countries.

This system depends on open borders and no tax to specific nations. Naturally, President Trump, who wants to reinforce national borders becomes an annoying enemy. Trump seeks to reinstate the national sovereignty of the United States, return jobs to the working class and rebuild America. Will he succeed?

China and the super-rich oligarchs in the West have joined forces and benefit massively from the globalist system. Or, to rephrase the sentence: The rise of China has fueled the rise of the Western oligarch super-rich elite, who bypass the Western worker and produce goods in cheap labor countries without redistributing wealth back to the West. And due to the implementation of open borders and no tax paid to specific nations, most companies are registered in tax havens.[iii]

It is problematic that the mainstream media, owned by the super-rich, has increasingly become a smoke screen that disguises these real driving forces that determine the development in the West.

Socialism provides, as we shall see, a strict totalitarian social control and cohesion among the population, so that its Marxist elite can do whatever they want, since the people have lost their personal freedom and are heavily subjected to the consensus of public propaganda. We saw the partnership between socialism and the capitalist industrial elite in Germany under Hitler, it worked very well.

It may be argued that freedom becomes, in a socialist system, the right to agree with the Marxist elite who have joined forces with the robbery capitalist owners. The rebel journalist and author, Karl Marx' detested religion, traditional values, historical Western ideals and its bourgeoisie. When reading him, the question becomes: Did Karl Marx really aim to help the working class in a proletariat class struggle, or was the idea simply to replace one ruling class with a new ruling elite – the Marxist tyrants?

This is what came full circle during the neo-Marxist revolution in the 1960s, and the radical hippies later took power over the media, the publishing houses, the universities, and public discourse. Communism, Marxism, National Socialism, and neo-Marxism as found in the 1960s New Left are all variations of the same ideology.

Neo-Marxism is defined as the post-war Marxist ideology that later was pushed by the New Left into Western societies, deconstructing traditional Western values such as the family, the church with its focus on personal responsibility and duties with the aim of redefining Western values in line with borderlessness, hedonism and Identity Politics.

From this neo-Marxist pool of thought grew the current next generation Antifa rebel groups that now cause havoc in the United States, as we shall see. As much as I detest addressing individuals by using the term for their skin color, it is needed in this book, due to the fervent Leftwing Identity Politics' focus on ethnic origin. I use the term "black" and "white" and "Afro-American" where it is a point in the argument to do so.

The Corona scandal has added speed to the Western middle class business owners being annihilated in the high-tech revolution owned by, for example Amazon and the world's richest man, the brilliant Jeff Bezos, who bypasses the local stores and businesses and reaches the customer directly.[iv]

The globalist capitalists –most are all socialists and leftwing in the United States – partner with low cost China and produce the death of the middle class in the West. And the working class. No wonder they fight Donald Trump who aims at halting this enrichment process and returning the manufacturing jobs to Americans and the respect for national sovereignty in the United States.

There are obvious pros and cons. We are in the middle of an economic revolution in which great business minds, such as that of Jeff Bezos, the founder of Amazon, makes books, clothes and items available to all without ever entering a shop. It arrives straight from China and other producing nations. The Covid-19 world crisis has but added benefits to this process, as people are forced to remain at home, shopping on Amazon. Which is great. Even this book is a testament to the Amazon brilliance and exquisite service and handling of customers that revolutionize the West as we speak.

As production was outsourced to China and the East, jobs were nonetheless lost in the West. Without redistribution of wealth, even Amazon may face loss in revenue as Westerners go bankrupt and cannot afford to purchase the wished for goods. There needs to be a free market for the smartest to operate, yet still, we need a population with sufficient purchasing power.

The chapter you are about to read, cover these topics from various angles and analyze some of the consequences of the current war between the Republican President Trump and the Democrats. It is not a comprehensive outlook aimed at providing a full overview, but rather selected commentaries on some American current affairs, focusing on what Trump has accomplished, his actions and stated values.

Clearly President Donald Trump is no saint, but he has, since he first decided to run for the presidency, stated his wish to rebuild America by focusing on national sovereignty and the return of jobs for Americans. And work for a just trade agreement with China. Since the mainstream media notoriously focuses negatively on Trump, I shall do the opposite in order to provide some balance to the full picture.

The aim of these asserted articles is to offer information and viewpoints that might be useful in arriving at an understanding of the events of our time. I believe that the information comes from reliable sources but cannot guarantee the information to be free of mistakes and incorrect interpretations. As parts of the argument addresses the same issues as in my book *New Left Tyranny. The Authoritarian Destruction of our Way of Life*, some segments will remind the reader about points also made there. I also quote parts of the Christian preacher and martyr, Dr. Martin Luther King Jr.'s letter from the Birmingham jail in order to place attention on his work and values, which is more important than ever.

Sources are cited as end note links to make it easier for the reader to further access more information. The articles are to be used as pieces of information that should be considered as part of the bigger picture when seeking to acquire a full overview regarding these specific subjects.

CHAPTER 2

Marxist China Spearheaded the Lockdowns

This is mysterious, indeed. The Sars' Coronavirus (Covid-19) has so far delivered fewer deaths than most yearly influenzas, yet the media frenzy is all time high. Truth is, we will all get it, almost. 60-80 % of the population will get the Corona virus, says British authorities.

A short summary of the regular seasonal influenza numbers demonstrates yearly losses of lives in the hundreds of thousands. As sad as it is, those among us who are old, frail and have serious illnesses or weaknesses leave this earth every year. With Covid-19 it is no different, therefore the regular influenza numbers matter. Yet very few media outlets compared the numbers when the Corona fear first erupted.

650 000 people[v] die yearly from respiratory illnesses linked to regular influenzas, according to the WHO.[vi] The US numbers for yearly deaths due to regular flus are, as CNN reported in 2018 around 80 000 dead yearly.[vii] Compared to the early Chinese numbers from Corona, the 2018 US influenza was much more pandemic.[viii] Yet, no media pumped that story up back then.

So, who first pushed for the lockdown strategy in the West and managed to sway opinion in that direction? Is the Corona epidemic being used politically? The question is of utmost relevance. It was China that set the example for lockdown of national economies in an unprecedented move.[ix]

Western nations followed the Chinese example and shut down their own economies too. Not lack of supply or demand halted growth, but political decisions. We are consequently facing the financial meltdown of a century by political choice.

China is now world leader, spearheading how everyone handles pandemic crisis. What the Marxist-Leninist President of the People's Republic, Xi Jinping does, we all follow and implement. Or do we?

Nobody seems to have noticed that China mainly closed down one city, Wuhan and its province, Hubei.[x] 5 million Wuhan inhabitants were allowed to leave and travelled elsewhere in China, which leaves 6 million in lockdown Wuhan.[xi]

By March 14, most of Hubei were to resume work and production. That means a lock down for approximately four weeks in most of Hubei. Other areas were also affected, national borders and so on.[xii]

The point being, that China only closed down epicenter areas, but the West closed down whole nations, counties, towns, municipalities, everywhere. This has severely impacted the economy on a level that may be far worse than China.

From day one, I suggested that the corona crisis must be seen in light of the US-China trade war.[xiii] It seems that the Western globalist worship of oligarchs now gives China the upper hand.

The panic advice to shut down came from a mix between oligarch Bill Gates,[xiv] WHO leader, Marxist-Leninist Dr. Tedros Adhanom Ghebreyesus[xv] and was massively pushed by the CNN led media.[xvi] Western oligarch owned CNN is actually proud of spearheading panic, they even summed it up in a CNN article.[xvii]

The Director-General of the World Health Organization, Dr. Tedros first under- then over reporting is central, since Western leaders believe that the WHO is the "equivalent to God".[xviii] He allegedly under reported the China numbers, then brutally switched to over reporting prospects of millions of dead on March 10th, to EU leaders.[xix]

In the March 10 meeting, he estimated 3.5 % or more death rates among the infected, describing the outbreak as "pandemic," millions dead in Europe. Apparently, Angela Merkel was so shocked that others had to calm her down.

An estimated 60-70 % in the population were expected to contract the virus. British authorities stated 60-80 %. By March 12, the EU closed down its economies.

This combined with, in essence, the Imperial College draft, caused the fear of a bug on a level never seen before. As it turns out, the Imperial College Report[xx] that motivated the UK and other nations to leave its herd immunity strategy, turns out to not be peer-reviewed and written by a professor

Neil Ferguson who highly overestimated the numbers for Ebola and Swine influenza.[xxi] It predicted that 510 000 could die in the UK without lockdown, while 250 000 could die even with an isolationist strategy.[xxii]

This was recently pointed out by Johan Giesecke,[xxiii] the State Epidemiologist for Sweden who also served as the first Chief Scientist of the European Centre for Disease Prevention and Control (ECDC).[xxiv]

We currently have politicians who eagerly flock around billionaire "pandemic expert," Bill Gates to take his oligarch advice rather than to listen to national pandemic experts.

Stanford School of Medicine professor John Ioannidis says that the lockdowns could be a "once in a century evidence fiasco."[xxv] He has described the coronavirus as a "very common, mild infection for the vast majority."[xxvi]

Do we know enough to justify the massive measures that violate human rights in our free democratic society, asks Germany's forefront virus expert in microbiology, Dr. Sucharit Bhakdi's open letter to the Chancellor of Germany? Of course, Merkel does not listen to him.[xxvii]

Dr. Bhakdi says: "This is the incredible tragedy. The life expectancy of millions is now being shortened because of this. The horrifying impact on world economy threatens the existence of countless people."[xxviii]

1.1 billion people are now threatened by hunger due to world-wide lockdowns. In the UK alone, three million go hungry.[xxix] Many are asking if the Covid-19 reaction was overblown. In that case, who pushed the exaggerations?

If politically motivated, the misinformation may have contributed to the largest economic meltdown in a century. Let us at least now stop continuing the sosio-economic suicide and get back to work.

CHAPTER 3

China and the Media is Selling us Fear?

Did American globalists end up joining the US-China trade war, helping China push even more media fear of Corona, simply to try to get to Trump? This since Russia Gate, impeachment and nothing else has worked? Ask Joe Biden or Nancy Pelosi. The horrendous outcomes may have been anticipated or unanticipated, but the results remain the same.[xxx]

The United States is now locked in an economic civil war over who is to own the country, its assets and global trade.[xxxi] President Trump has, from the beginning, spoken of national interest, jobs back to American workers, internationalist corporations paying taxes again, halting the monopoly structures that quench local businesses, reinstating the respect for the Constitution with its profound respect for the Judeo-Christian values. And establish fair trade with China that also benefits the U.S. working class.

The globalist model of acquiring the world's wealth assembled in the hands of the top elite was at stake from the very second Trump was chosen. The globalists who also own the media have attempted for years to remove Trump - Russia

Gate, impeachment and so on. By fueling the media with fear, yet another attempt on Trump is on the way.

In the 2020 financial melt-down, it seems that the globalists have jointed China in attacking the US economy. This is a new chapter in the US - China trade war, with empty shelves all across the West soon to be filled by Chinese products. It is a government ordered shutdown of Western economy, not determined by lack of demand. The West is under siege by a cunning enemy.

The current economic crisis arguably has three components: The falling oil price due to the slowing down of the Chinese economy. Russia's no to OPEC+ took a hit at US shale oil and helped spur low oil prices of which the rise of China is dependent.[xxxii]

Saudi Arabia is increasing their production, China as main customer. Number two: The fear of death from the Corona virus.[xxxiii] Number three: The enhancing of this fear coming from the globalist owners of the Western media in order to finally "get to Trump".[xxxiv]

As the Chinese markets fell due to the outbreak, stocks plunged and the China government allegedly responded by buying up stocks and nationalizing assets. Reportedly, they are now doing the same in the financial crisis.

It was at this point that China's President Xi Jinping[xxxv] used the term "a devil" about the virus.[xxxvi] Those who have studied Confucianism know exactly what it implies pertaining to Chinese fury. "Xi's terminology is a major clue. He said, on the record, that this was war. And, as a counter-attack, a "people's war" had to be launched," writes political analyst Pepe Escobar.[xxxvii]

Here is a key piece of information that few comment on: This was right after President Trump signed the fair trade agreement with China back in January, 2019, correcting currency manipulation and intellectual property laws.[xxxviii]

The Chinese may have felt that they lost face. Two weeks later, news of the Corona erupted amid record low unemployment in the US. Much to the distress of CNN who together with its mainstream media owners have tried to crush Trump for years.[xxxix]

Ironically, CNN now confirm the massive Trump gains since he took office, the same gains that CNN formerly denied, only now in order to demonize how the market crash hurts Trump. It is remarkable how undisclosed intentions are on display in the current US mainstream media. They are still happy to hurt Trump, even if it takes the whole country down.

CHAPTER 4

The Panic Fear of Corona is the Worst Enemy

The panic fear of the Covid-19 may be the very element that brought about major economic decline and restructuring of ownership all across the West.

So, why does the media push such panic over Corona, even considering the sad fact that many die, but not over regular flus that kill hundreds of thousands more?[xl] Who will profit from the Corona panic as the economy plunges and massive bankruptcies require new owners and new liquidity to the market?

The psychology of the fear of Corona has so far produced the worst market crash in recent history, maybe ever. The media hype is key. Do the owners of the mainstream press have market interests? Oxfam numbers show around 60 individuals own over 50 % of world assets, will we see ten individuals own it post-Corona?

In Italy, which has Europe's oldest population, thousands die yearly from flus, 68 000 died of various flus between 2013-2017, according to one study.[xli] Over 5 million got the illness. We never heard much about that.

Corona may reportedly be viewed as mostly dangerous to the elderly or those who already suffer from respiratory illnesses. Risk lies in the capacity of the heath service to handle respiratory complex treatment. The number of Corona deaths could, of course rise to massive counts.

The average age of those dying from Corona is 79.5 years old, 70 % men, most of whom have two or three other serious diagnosis.[xlii]

Israel, with its well informed intelligence, took the correct response by reducing the panic, isolating its elderly and prone to respiratory illnesses, implementing social distance while the national economy continued.[xliii]

Korea seems to have beaten the virus, demonstrating its discipline and collective approach by implementing social distance, protecting the elderly and business carry-on. Let us take down the Corona virus, not our economies, was the mantra.

The illness was not unknown even in March 2020, as China, Korea, Singapore and others already had been through the curve. Pr. March 15th, China reported, according to Worldometer, a total of 80.849 sick from Corona, 3.199 dead and 66.931 recovered, six to eight weeks peak. Even considering Chinese under reporting, the numbers are still very low. Whoever owns the vaccine, is of course set to earn billions.

The US and the United Kingdom initially chose different approaches from the EU to the emergence of the Corona flu.[xliv] On the continent and in Scandinavian countries such as Norway, Denmark, panicking political leaders were among the first to "obey the WHO" and choose full economic shutdown of restaurants, barber shops, retail, almost everything except food stores. This pushed the nations into a massive break-down of their economies and a brutal recession.

The US and the UK initially stressed the need to keep business running and daily life open as long as possible, targeting high risk groups. This is the so-called herd immunity strategy.[xlv] The UK national emergency plan focused on the most endangered, on equipping hospitals, avoiding contact, keeping business open, the country now flooding with respiratory masks.

Prime minister, Boris Johnson prescribes caution and the need to consider avoiding plunging the country into even deeper troubles. This was before the Imperial Report hit the Prime minister's desk and both the US and the UK changed their approach.

The EU choice of total shut down of the economy was a conspicuously quick response, that produced a much worse economic recession. The massive recession ahead all across the West and the world as a whole, brutally enhanced by government's panic shutdown of daily life, will result in catastrophic bankruptcies, hunger and millions of lost jobs.

The result will, in a few months, be a massive shift of ownership as the back of the old system is broken. As Wall Street restructuring companies now slip into the already muddy waters, we are set to see a new world where the smartest take it all.

As panic sets in, precisely the shut-down of shops and industries over a virus that has not caused even the same amount of deaths that regular influenzas do, may prove to be the very worst irresponsible action, much worse than the Corona itself. It may mark yet another ending point of Western hegemony, as Russia quietly celebrates a very low debt rate with a highly competitive oil industry, and China is on the rise post-Corona.

CHAPTER 5

The Push for Lockdown by Billionaire Bill Gates and WHO

It may be argued that the Coronavirus scandal, with billionaire oligarch "pandemic expert" Bill Gates pushing horror scenarios into the media, strongly contributed to politicians' reaction of fear. This, combined with mass media hysteria, has in turn, caused a once-in-a-century financial depression.

At The Herland Report we suggested early[xlvi] that the crisis should be seen in relation to the current U.S.-China trade war. We wrote about the topic of World Health Organization leader, Dr. Tedros' possible politization the *day before* President Trump addressed it. Two days later it was headlines across the world.[xlvii]

The close relationship between Dr. Tedros and Bill Gates is illustrated by Tedros calling Gates "my brother" when opening speeches. Everyone else, such as the WHO-favored Norwegian prime minister, Erna Solberg, are addressed as dignitaries. Through its CEPI work, the current Norwegian government have been allied with Gates,[xlviii] Norway funding billions into vaccine programs.[xlix]

Non-elected Western billionaire oligarchs attempt to rule us now, Bill Gates forefront as the "pandemic expert." Through the Davos system, private capital merges with lucrative government funds, causing the rise of oligarchs replacing democratic rule of nation states. Global private capital has an unprecedented access to taxpayer money.

Gates owns everything from charity to world vaccines, pays the WHO by the billions, funds NGOs and controls politicians who treat him like a king from the Middle Ages.[l] He owns medical facilities, controls distribution channels and medical staff, owns the research, the vaccines, the health institutes, and was recently criticized by Robert Kennedy for his "messianic complex." Just talk to Elon Musk.[li]

It is a massive problem that non-democratically elected Bill Gates shapes our democracies with "philanthropist" billions. Gates pushed the idea of the pandemic of the century.[lii] He even suggested in a recent interview, that the opening up[liii] should not come until there is a digital immune proof documenting who is vaccinated or not.[liv] The vaccine would be Gates owned, w assume.

So, our nations should be shut down for months, destroying Western economies completely? This year's U.S. Center for Disease Control and Prevention numbers estimate that, as of mid-March, between 29,000 and 59,000 have died due to regular influenza illnesses.[lv] Nobody compares these numbers to COVID-19's related 21.000 deaths in the same period.[lvi]

Note that the correct numbers are hard to estimate, as the U.S. now allows suspicion of Coronavirus to be enough for medical personnel to state it as the cause of death.[lvii] Dr.

Anthony Fauci and two co-authors published a letter on March 26, 2020 in the New England Journal of Medicine. Dr. Fauci is the Director of the National Institute of Allergy and Infectious Diseases.

In the article, linked below, he states that COVID-19 may turn out to be comparable in numbers of deaths to a seasonal flu or similar to two relatively minor flu pandemics in 1957 and 1968, the Patriot Fire wrote.[lviii]

The Institute for Health Metrics and Evaluation (IHME) estimated around about 72,000 deaths in the US from Covid-19 in 2020. Yet, seasonal flu killed 80.000 in 2018, as we have seen.

So many have spoken of the danger in not allowing the establishment of herd immunity. The need to protect the old and the medically frail is key, without destroying the economy. Dr. Knut Wittkowski, Rockefeller University New York, said in an interview[lix] that the isolation policies could result in more deaths in the long term, writes Daily Wire.[lx] Lockdown prolongs efforts in developing herd immunity among the population.

The alarming interview with Germany's forefront virus expert in microbiology and a world authority on the subject, Dr. Sucharit Bhakdi, sends a chillingly apocalyptic message: that the Western government shutdown is a completely wrong and extremely dangerous response to COVID-19.

He says that self-isolating the whole population is "grotesque, absurd and very dangerous. All these measures are leading to self-destruction and collective suicide caused by fear."[lxi]

Nobody listens to Dr. Bhakdi or Dr. Wittkowski, as we have world leader and "pandemic expert" Bill Gates all over every news channel. For the first time in history, lack of supply or demand did not shut down the economy and create a depression. State leaders forced the shutdown on their own nations, local businesses, industries, corporations, and employers. The situation is unprecedented in history.[lxii]

CHAPTER 6

Stop the Socioeconomic Suicide

Many are now openly asking if the Covid-19 reaction was overblown, and in that case, who pushed the exaggerations? If politically motivated, the misinformation suggesting mass deaths has contributed to the largest economic meltdown in a century.

Not lack of supply or demand halted growth, but political decisions. We are consequently facing the financial meltdown of a century by political choice.

"You have a 0.03% chance of dying from COVID in the state of California. Does that necessitate people being out of work," asked Accelerated Urgent Care owner, Dr. Dan Erickson recently.[lxiii]

He showed how the Covid-19 has taken very few lives in the state of California, questioning the continued economic lockdowns. The question is legitimate, as China – whom we all seem to follow in their spearheading of lockdowns – only closed down its epicenter, Wuhan and parts of the Hubei province.

Dr. Dan Erickson and Dr. Artin Massihi urged the California government to lift the extreme measures. Tesla CEO Elon Musk, retweeted, "Docs make good points."

They compared the Covid-19 to an influenza with millions of cases, but small amounts of death. The death rate for California turns out to be approximately 0.03 %, in line with the Rystad Energy estimates and others. Rystad reports that as of 27 April, 54 million people have likely been infected with Covid-19.[lxiv]

"It is now clear that the lockdowns were a major mistake everywhere except the New York City metro area, and possibly even there," said former New York Times reporter Alex Berenson.[lxv]

The Imperial College Report, which showed that millions would die, was central to make the UK and US change their herd immunity strategy. The report has since turns out to be fraudulent, its author Neil Ferguson sacked and the entire report not even peer reviewed. Ferguson was notorious for overestimating numbers, both during the Ebola and Swine flu. Ferguson estimated that 150 000 would die in the UK during the Foot and Clove flu. 200 died.[lxvi]

As it turns out, Dr. Anthony Fauci now reportedly says that it was he and Dr. Blix who came into President Trump's office and made him change his mind about herd immunity, allegedly based on the Imperial Report.[lxvii]

It seem then, that it was Dr. Fauci who persuaded the President to shut down, which effectively has stopped the soaring US economy. They allegedly did this based on the Imperial College Report, which said millions would die from Coronavirus in the United States.

As many as 1 100 000 died from smoking in the same time period as Covid-19, according to Worldometer info.[lxviii] 2 million died from cancer in the same period, and as much as 2.4 million from hunger. Bill Gates, WHO and CNN saw no need to sound the alarm on that.[lxix]

1.1 billion now risk starvation due to the extreme lockdown measures. In the UK alone, 3 million go hungry due to lockdown, according to a recent report.[lxx]

The narrative has become that of either "caring for the people" and remaining in lockdown or caring "only for the economy and money" and reopening. This ill-advised narrative prevents politicians from reopening, although they know this to be the right move.

The economy *is* the well-being of the people. With a destroyed economy, mass unemployment and bankruptcies, there is no healthy people, only national suffering. This seems to be the chosen path.

Trump as the Enemy Godfather of the American Mafia

CHAPTER 7

Trump - The New Enemy of the American Mafia?

In order to examine the broader picture, let us turn to the drug epidemic in the United States. It ruins millions of lives. Who benefits from this billion-dollar revenue business? A remarkable element in President Trump's first TV address to the nation from the Oval Office, in the stand-off with Congress that led to a 18 day partial government shutdown, was his blunt attack on the current billion dollar drug mafia in America.[lxxi]

It is quite a puzzle. Why does the mainstream media discourage President Trump's fight against illegal activity along US borders? Who profits from open borders if not the American drug cartels whose criminal activity is dependent on illegal access to the US?

Who profits from human trafficking? In whose interest is it to push for an illegal immigration that lowers the wages of unskilled workers and keeps the billion-dollar drug industry running? And why does the Democratic Party so fervently support the illegal activity that produces anarchy in the US?

To cite Greg Gutfeld, President Trump addressed "the 266,000 arrests of aliens with criminal records, The 100,000 assaults, the 30,000 sex crimes, the 4,000 violent killings, the 1 in 3 women sexually assaulted on the trek through Mexico, the 20,000 migrant children illegally brought into the U.S. last month."[lxxii]

The 1930's Chicago controlling Mafia seem innocent compared to the drug cartels that run this business in the USA today. Back then, the Mafioso bosses ordered the killings of individuals who opposed their illegal activities in the entertainment industry, drugs, prostitution, gambling and so on.

Who are the Mafioso controlling America today? As the President pointed out, the illegal drug trade is a wide and national epidemic. Somebody high up profits by the billions.

It is well known that the drug industry has exploded in the West, Afghanistan alone now counting for over 90 % of the production of heroin, with massive growth after US takeover.[lxxiii] "Thirty years too late" comes a President who wants to deal with today's American drug lords, yet somehow the mainstream media supports the criminal activity along the Southern borders, or at least, does not want to stop it.

The market for illegal drugs in the United States is about $100 billion each year, according to a RAND study. 27 million Americans are on illicit drugs. 7 out of 10 Americans are on prescription drugs, according to the Mayo Clinic.

Drug abuse in America is at its all-time high, constituting an epidemic of immense proportions. According to DrugWarFacts.org, as of 2014, over 27 million Americans1, aged 12 or older, were current illicit drug users, reported Boulevard Treatment Center.

As President Trump wants to close the US southern border where most of this is transported into the US and gain control over the human trafficking, drug import, entry of illegal aliens and other criminal activity, the mainstream media fights his efforts to accomplish this. Why? Who profits from this trade?

Ironically, it is the Democratic Party that fights for the rights of the super-rich. The Speaker of the House and Democrat, whose mother came from the notorious Southern Italy, Nancy Pelosi of California, even pronounced Trump's border wall "an immorality", to which Democrats cheered and agreed.

Pelosi knows perfectly well that the flow of immigrants enter the US illegally and against US law, that their presence push the current wage-level down,[lxxiv] that the legal immigrants voted for Trump[lxxv] to stop the illegal immigration.[lxxvi] Who has conveniently managed to sway Pelosi from supporting local, legal workers to fighting *for criminal activity*?

The basic question is: In whose interest is it to *not* make America safe? Who profits from anarchy and sub-groups in society fighting in this age of Identity Politics? Who profits from the millions of young Americans on narcotics, sold outside schools, given to children? And who profits from the lowering of wages and the disruption of civil society?

One of the dramatic effects of illegal immigration is that the wages are pushed down. The illegal and unskilled immigrants gladly work for lower wages and are easily exploited.[lxxvii]

Statistics show that a high number of legal immigrants voted for Trump,[lxxviii] many stating that the reason was his announced-to-be crack-down on illegal immigration.[lxxix] One may argue that the globalist, transnational agenda pushes for lower wages in the US, and illegal immigration through its Southern borders is vital to attain this goal.[lxxx]

What we are witnessing is a historic show down of power between the New World Order globalist, transnational elite and the Old-World Order that wants to retain national borders and the sovereignty of nations. Finally comes a President who fights for the law abiding and hard-working citizens in the attempt to rebuild American strength.

CHAPTER 8

We Criticize Trump, Yet Build Our Own Walls

The European hypocrisy when criticizing President Donald Trump's efforts to stop illegal immigration along the US' southern border, simply is baffling. Not to mention that the building of the border wall to Mexico was begun under the leadership of Barack Obama.[lxxxi] The so-called cages in which minors were placed, were also built under the Obama era.[lxxxii]

The European mainstream media are tripping over themselves in copying *New York Times* and *Washington Post* attitudes of demonizing the "racist" Trump efforts to build a wall to stop criminal activity, none of them mentioning that Europe already has its own walls.

The criminal activity include the multi-billion dollar drug epidemic trail[lxxxiii] into the US, ten billion dollars of drugs[lxxxiv] goes annually through Arizona alone. [lxxxv] Unbelievable 99.8 % of illegal drugs[lxxxvi] are shipped into the US through the Mexico border. 64 billion USD worth of drugs[lxxxvii] are sent into the US every year from Mexico. The Democrats fight like crazy to maintain it.

Yet, the European Union already built their own wall.[lxxxviii] Billions have been allocated to maintain the exact same type of wall, between Turkey and Syria.[lxxxix] It is 764 kilometer (475 mile) long, designed to keep illegal Asians from flooding Turkey and from there, travelling into Europe.

Turkish forces reportedly fire machine guns on the refugees who are trying to cross the border, blocking them from entering, as reported by Human Rights Watch.[xc] The German Der Spiegel[xci] has a quite revealing article on the issue. In addition, the EU is allegedly funding[xcii] the military equipment used to stop the illegal refugees from entering Turkey, according to quite an extensive report by The Black Sea.[xciii]

The deals risk the EU being complicit in possible violations of the international rights of refugees. Still no mainstream European media outlet touches the subject. All they ever talk about is “the horribly racist Trump wall”.

The EU funded wall in Turkey reportedly incorporates both electronic and advanced technology layers. The physical layer includes modular concrete walls, patrol routes, manned and unmanned towers and passenger tracks, according to one of the few media outlets that address this issue.[xciv]

When Hungarian prime minister ,Viktor Orbán – sworn enemy of Open Society, globalist hedge fund manager, George Soros - made the fence that stops the flow of migrants into Europe in Hungary, the media outcry was immense.[xcv] Orbán was “racist, islamophobe, anti-Europe, anti-immigrants” and so on. Yet, later, when the EU funds a 764-kilometer wall between Turkey and Syria, the media is remarkably silent.

The European Commission Fact Sheet report from 2016 states that EU would, in close cooperation with Turkey, allocated €3 billion under the Facility for Refugees and speed it up.[xcvi]

An additional €3 billion will be allocated to Turkey by the end of 2018. Part of the deal was also opening up the borders between Turkey and the EU. No one can deny that Turkey's Erdogan is brilliant. He makes the whole of Europe sing in fear to his tune, while being paid billions for it.

According to Der Spiegel: "The EU states have provided the government in Ankara with security and surveillance technology valued at more than 80 million euros in exchange for the protection of its borders."[xcvii]

It is perfectly understandable that countries try to prevent illegal immigration, as it destabilizes the nation, creates anarchy and has all kinds of destructive effects. Not the least, it tends to push the wage level down,[xcviii] which benefits the ultra-rich,[xcix] as pointed out by many, among them the US best-selling author and social commentator, Ann Coulter.[c]

National borders are there to prevent chaos and make sure its citizens have rights, prosperity, and legal protection. Since the Westphalia Peace in 1648, national sovereignty has been the core principle to peace between nations.

Those who continuously push for a capitalist globalization of markets and therefore need open and unregulated borders, understandably need to demolish national sovereignty. The internationalist economic system is dependent on borderless societies to dominate the world stage. They want the few to succeed, not for the rising wage levels for the broad parts of the people. #Davos.

The Liberal-Progressive morality probably goes like this: When President Trump does it, it's automatically wrong and should be condemned in the harshest way possible. When the Europeans do exactly the same, we all support it.

When the Obama administration points out that the southern border represents serious threats,[ci] as Todd Bensman at Middle East Forum reports,[cii] the media remains silent.

If "white, male, heterosexual" Trump says illegal immigration is dangerous, he automatically is a racist, to allude to a The Herland Report interview with Dr. Paul Craig Roberts on the topic of the Identity Politics' hatred against the white, heterosexual male.[ciii]

The European hypocrisy, both in the media and among politicians, is astounding. We exemplify the art of double standards in an unprecedented manner.

CHAPTER 9

The Pettiest Female in America: Nancy Pelosi

Rudeness, a total lack of civility and respect for democracy - the people's vote seems to permeate the Democrat view in the United States. One of the latest and saddest examples, were to be seen on full display as President Donald Trump held his State of the Union Address in 2019.[civ]

I urge all women not to follow the example of what must be the rudest, lowest female in public America, Speaker of the House, Nancy Pelosi. The utterly disgraceful display of lack of manners as she tore up the President's comments makes me ashamed to be a woman.[cv]

Pelosi takes the lead as one of the most prominent women in the media. We respect that at the height of her career, she decided to take the risk of impeaching a President. It is quite a bold movement, which she lost. Taking the public lead also makes her a role model for millions. She should lead a life as an example, not tarnish our female reputation by such a display of rudeness and lack of respect for the presidency.

It does not matter whether she likes Donald Trump or not. The State of the Union Address is an official occasion that unifies America under one President. Pelosi's first mistake was being utterly unable, as many women sadly are, to distinguish between personal sentiment and official duty.

The demonstrative rudeness and uncivilized lack of respect for the presidency during the Address must mark one of the lowest points in Pelosi's career. If you have no joy to display when the speaker informs you of the lowest unemployment rate in history among blacks, you still smile and clap. That is being a professional. If you have grudges against the speaker, you address those at another and appropriate occasion.

This President was elected by the American people, according to US law. Even after the massive impeachment circus, his approval rating is at a record-high 49 percent, according to a fresh Gallup poll.[cvi]

Even worse than the lack of professionalism, Pelosi's actions demonstrated that she does not care about the betterment of the American people. Instead of rising above the current political strife and celebrate the rising living standards, record low unemployment, an economic boom which has launched millions out of poverty, she did not clap. Nor rise, just rudely flipped with papers.

When Trump spoke about America being pro-worker, pro-family, pro-growth, and, most of all, pro-American, she did not rise nor clap. Does Pelosi disagree with the President on this as a national goal? Probably, or else she would have clapped.

When he spoke of the United States lifting high citizens of every race, color, religion, and creed, she did not clap nor rise. She disagrees with him on that too?

What happened to America since such women are its proudest display of female power? Is it not the very core of political work to make sure that the population prospers? Not for Pelosi. She saw no reason to clap for the end of American economic decline.

When Trump spoke of the rise of the working class, she showed no joy. It is obviously not on Pelosi's agenda to be happy about the *blue-collar boom*. She took the time to clean her teeth, fix her hair, demonstratively not showing support for the record low black unemployment. Mike Pence got up and celebrated. At least, Americans now know who is happy about the economic rise and who just couldn't be bothered.

This is why we need men. Their ability to rise above personal sentiments, division, quarrels based on slander and allegations, the ability to not care about petty rumors, but stand firm and perform in the office they hold.

Why do women so often seem susceptible to the low life urge to speak evil of others? They just can't get over their own, inner ocean of ramped up cluttered, personal feelings.

To us Europeans, the display of rudeness and utter stupidity is probably the worst. Does Pelosi not understand that she displays a complete lack of respect for democracy itself by remaining silent when such national accomplishments are being listed up?

By refraining from clapping upon hearing about the millions out of poverty under the economic boom, does she not comprehend that she shows contempt for the same millions of blue collar, working class individuals? The speech ended by Pelosi by ripping up Trump comments. Which PR expert advised such an action? She should be fired.

Pelosi is, of course already notorious for openly explaining how Democrats smear, lie and defame their opponents with the "wrap up smear." It sadly speaks for the character.[cvii] She remarkably open told members of the press in what must have been an unguarded moment, how the Democratic Party smears its opponents with falsehoods and lies, then reports the smear and lies to the press.

They further use the same smear - reported in the press by themselves, as Pelosi says, to re-validate the lies as "confirmed by the press." It is apparently called The Wrap Up Smear, of which she proudly confident tells is a party tactic.

To cite Pelosi: "You demonize, it is called the Wrap Up Smear. You smear somebody, with falsehoods and all the rest. Then you merchandize it, you write it and say "It is reported in the press" this and this, so you have the validation that the press reported the smear. That's what's called a Wrap Up Smear." So, we merchandize what the press has reported on the smear that we made. It is a tactic."[cviii]

Only to add to the obvious hypocrisy, House Speaker Pelosi was caught on camera visiting a San Francisco hair salon in August, 2020 to have her hair washed. This may not seem like it is newsworthy, but the local ordinances have kept salons closed for months during the coronavirus pandemic, destroying businesses and keeping many unemployed.

In security footage that was obtained by Fox News, the California congresswoman was seen walking through

ESalonSF in San Francisco with her wet hair. She does not have a mask covering her mouth or nose, which is required.

After besmirching Trump for not wearing a mask and attacking him for months about it, this doubt-standard of 'do what I say not what I do' smacks of the greatest hypocrisy. This was compounded even further the following day when Speaker Pelosi discovered she had been caught abusing her power and position, so she told the media that the shop owner had set her up. The Democratic play book of blaming the victim.[cix]

Let the end of American decline please include new female role models who do not push for civil war, rudeness and petty behavior, but are able to contain themselves, display virtues, sincerity, civility and female honorable grace.

CHAPTER 10

Billionaires Manipulate the Green and Greta Thunberg?

As politics and economy are intertwined in today's economic system, manipulating politics also means manipulating markets. The political Green Movement illustrates this deception to the max. As the billionaire funded, Wall Street supported Greta Thunberg, Climate Change, Apocalypse, Extinction Rebellion push demands divestment in oil, who is looking to gain when the shortage sets in?

At the center of attention are mainstream media loved Extinction Rebellion and Fossil Free[cx] - the group behind the public child abuse of Greta Thunberg.[cxi] The girl clearly has no idea that she serves Wall Street billionaires interests as a media puppet for a much broader game.

We live in a time of massive manipulations of politics from the financial industry. The media owners now also own the largest corporations in America. The media has become a political tool for the billionaires' next investments. Globalist politics, the socialist press and robbery-capitalism in Wall Street walk hand in hand these days.

Only four percent of world energy is currently provided by so-called Green energy, solar and windmills, according to

BP Statistical Review. 96 percent of world energy is provided by oil, gas, coal.

The leading Wall Street investors know that the world does not have any comparable source of energy than coal, oil and gas. Water, solar and wind is not, at its current stage of development, on any level able to compare in power intensity or solve the world's energy needs. Bill Gates recently also pointed this out.[cxii]

So, who is manipulating the world energy market through the billion-dollar reallocation of Wall Street funds combined with an apocalyptic end-of-the-world media deception with front runners such as the child Thunberg? The aim is to end investments in oil and gas world-wide. Who wants to shut down energy to create an upcoming shortage, only to earn billions when the tide turns?

The irony is that the world's leading hedge fund manager, long term known for manipulating markets, George Soros, is one of the main drivers behind the eco-friendly climate change organizations.

The Green movement has far wealthier sponsors than the local Swedish businessmen behind Greta Thunberg, Ingmar Renzhog[cxiii], and Fossil Free leader, Bo Thorén.[cxiv]

The climate change business is a trillion dollar industry.[cxv] The Heritage Foundation states[cxvi] that in 2012 alone, the leftwing Climate Policy Initiative study "Global investment in climate change" found that $359 billion was invested in eco-projects that year alone.[cxvii]

Here is the catch: George Soros' investments in oil, gas and coal far overshadow his[cxviii] investment in eco-groups.[cxix] He is not the only left-wing[cxx] billionaire donating to end oil[cxxi] and at the same time investing heavily in oil and gas.

The point is that the US billionaires profit from all of this: By controlling the fossil fuel sector through the Wall Street divestment in oil strategy, an energy shortage is created in the world.[cxxii] Once the shortage sets in, the very same investors will profit by the billions.[cxxiii]

Their army of Green youth, having worked for free or paid very little, will gain nothing, and simply return to school. None of them are likely to complain as most never even found out what happened. They would be happy that the world did not end in the much-anticipated apocalypse, created by their sectarian Green "religion", after all.

Another benefit that few speak about it, actually none as far as I have seen: the Wall Street billionaire take-over of local shale oil companies through the prolonged oil crisis which puts the small shale owners out of business as they are not able to pay back debts. US laws state that whoever finds shale on his property, owns it.[cxxiv]

Investors starve local shale drillers for funds, writes Wall Street Journal[cxxv] and Financial Times, underlying the squeeze of funding.[cxxvi] As hundreds of local shale oil companies - many with local owners - now are bankrupt, the billionaire owned, regular oil companies are ready to take over. As FT points out: Consolidation is under way.

The divestment strategy fuels the American economy, which needs low oil prices. Both the political Green movement, the Wall Street funded community awareness groups and active demonstrators such as Extinction Rebellion and Fossil Free, as well as the US trade war on China all boost low oil prices and thereby, the US economy. The United States' Central Bank, the Federal Reserve, is a privately owned business at its top levels, as most are aware of.[cxxvii]

CHAPTER 11

The Greta Thunberg Show: Public Child Abuse

The use children as bait to create media sympathy for various causes, is an increasingly used method in the West.[cxxviii] Latest, Swedish Greta Thunberg, a 16 year old, has been given the role as "media puppet for climate change."

When she spoke at the UN in 2019, she probably had no clue of the political game she is a useful tool for. The teenager was even nominated for the Nobel Peace Prize, which she might get one day judging on the politicized way that the Norwegian Nobel Committee picks its candidates.

Whomever is popular in the ultra-liberal mainstream media has, in recent years, also been awarded the Prize, disregarding the requirements stated in the will of Alfred Nobel.

Swedish Greta Thunberg apparently has a known past with mental issues, a diagnosis of Asperger's syndrome, high-functioning autism, depression, a history of self-starvation and obsessive compulsive disorder.[cxxix]

As it is not unusual that world leaders may have illnesses, the remarkable using of a child like Thunberg has been sad to watch. This is the child now pampered by power structures in society to travel the world with the mainstream media covering her every step as she gives apocalyptic speeches and end-of-the-world threats.

As the world searches for heroes, someone in powerful places has decided that Greta Thunberg is what we need.[cxxx] Let me guess it will remain that way for as long as Thunberg and her parents allow the abuse of the girl to continue. Once it is over, and she stops being useful to whoever is paying for all of this, we will never hear of her again.

The young girl initially found world fame by organizing school strikes in her hometown in Sweden, skipping school and demanding climate change to be taken seriously by the Western world leaders.

Then someone paid for the community organizing of similar protests in over a hundred cities and Thunberg was forefront at the World Economic Forum in Davos, in front of the British Parliament, at UN Climate Talks. After dropping school again, to travel the world and perform theatrical, angry speeches, one wonders what benefit it will bring her later in life.

The world truly has gone mad. Thunberg, now used by the politicized “climate change” industry is only 16. The child is allowed to give hysterical, rude talks about “the world at mass extinction, entire ecosystems collapsing, the end of the world stories.

“We are in the beginning of a mass extinction and all you can talk about is money and fairytales of eternal economic growth," to cite Daily Wire.[cxxxi] It is utter stupidity. Thunberg, for one, would not even be able to travel was it not for economic growth and billion-dollar wealth pushed into the very same industry she now is a poster child for. Who writes her speeches?[cxxxii] The guy should be fired.

The child is allowed to mockingly shout "how dare you" at the grown-ups in the UN assembly, who have to sit and listen to such rubbish simply because big money has paid for her very entrance.

The Swede simply displays a complete lack of manners typical of Western youth these days, - the millennial Antifas who shout obscenities in the faces of policemen and jump up and down like small children would do - which must shock many of the UN delegates who are honorable individuals in senior positions in their respectable countries.

The Thunberg story is a testament of the suicidal state that Western culture currently finds itself in, abusing a young child into such public embarrassment.

Let me predict that nobody will care what will happen to this child in later years, when Thunberg has outdone her use to the mainstream powers. Is this what we have become, so lightheartedly using her already frail destiny to achieve "sympathy" for a cause that already has billions of dollars in its pot?

Apparently Donald Trump who held a brilliant speech at the UN in 2019 is the poor child's enemy.[cxxxiii] She is aligned with the media owners, which tells you all you need to know about who pays for the Thunberg show. Everyone knows that

China and the Far East are the worst climate offenders, using coal and so on, yet of that Thunberg has nothing to say.

When the parents of another used child, the Syrian Boy, Omran Daqneesh, depicted in the iconic orange ambulance, protested against the use of his face, the media hardly reported it.[cxxxiv] The parents said to Lebanese media that they were furious that their son was abused by rebel groups who used his face in the international propaganda campaigns against Assad. The boy's face, for whom the CNN anchor and the whole world so famously cried, became iconic in Western media, to symbolize the brutality of the Assad regime as Aleppo fell.[cxxxv]

Whoever is responsible for the abuse of Greta, let him stop. Let her go home and finish her schooling and get a bright future in Sweden.

Trump, Racism and Marxist Revolution In America

CHAPTER 12

Marxist Black Lives Matter is against Democracy

Sadly, we find ourselves in a situation where the color of somebody's skin now seems to be necessary to mention. One may argue that this is the result of decades of New Left Identity Politics, which aims to construct the identity from its cultural connection to subgroups in society rather than what has been done historically, to national heritage.

The legacy of the Christian preacher and martyr, Dr. Martin Luther King Jr. (1929-1968), the forefront civil rights movement leader in the 1960s, seems to be long forgotten. He preached nonviolence, yet strong resistance against oppression.

His Christian message is obviously now out of fashion, as Marxist violent revolution is the chosen path among the Democrats in America. Dr. King was very clear on the problem of deep-rooted racism. In his letter from the Birmingham jail: "We know through painful experience that freedom is never voluntarily given by the oppressor; it must be demanded by the oppressed. Frankly, I have never yet engaged in a direct-action movement that was "well timed" according to the timetable of those who have not suffered unduly from the disease of segregation."[cxxxvi]

"If blacks today had a real leader like Martin Luther King Jr., that leader would be protesting police violence against *people irrespective of race. Such a protest would be a unifying act instead of a divisive one.* People such as myself could again see hope for American society,» writes Dr. Paul Craig Roberts at The Herland Report.[cxxxvii]

As raging crowds now erupt all over the United States, community organizing obviously paid for by others than the kids and criminals rioting in the streets, I support black lives and the fight against racism, but not the Marxist, anti-democracy anarchist Black Lives Matter (BLM) movement.

Since they recently explained that they are trained Marxists whose goal it is to remove the democratically elected President in the United States, they lost my respect.[cxxxviii] Sadly so, because the fight against racism, defined as judging someone solely based on the color of their skin, is deeply disturbing and does not produce a just society with freedom for all.

The BLM Global Network co-founder, Patrisse Cullors, recently said to CNN: "Trump should resign now. Trump needs to be out of office. He is not fit for office. And so, what we are going to push for is a move to get Trump out."[cxxxix]

Black Lives Matter thereby states that the organization is against the rule of the people.[cxl] If the goal is to implement authoritarian dictatorship in a Marxist revolution, it is anti-democratic and anti-American in essence.

How exactly is a Marxist dictatorship going to help the black communities in the US? Have we lost all knowledge about what happened in the Soviet Union, the Gulag or the Holocaust?

The demonizing of certain ethnic groups, as if good and evil corresponds to skin color, is precisely what the Communist and National Socialist (NAZI) systems implemented. Millions of Jews, Gypsies, intellectuals and gays were killed by Hitler. Ask George Soros about it, he was there.

Is Hitler's race orientation the role model for Black Lives Matter? Communist Antifa pushes for the same Marxist goal.[cxli] The millennial black clad mainly white youth are educated at American Universities that have preached neo-Marxism 1960s hatred of traditional,[cxlii]historical Western values for decades now.[cxliii]

Read about this in my book *The Culture War. How the West lost its Freedom*, available at Amazon and across 60 nations.[cxliv] No wonder they vote for Karl Marx' bloody revolution.[cxlv] Are they paid by China or globalists?

Antifa claims to oppose "fascism," but fascism is defined by Webster's Dictionary as a totalitarian governmental system led by a dictator. Donald Trump is democratically elected by the majority of Americans. He is not a dictator, so Antifa are not fighting fascism. Who told them, by the way, that they are fighting against fascism? Clearly, Antifa millennials do not even know what the term means.

The remarkably "white millennial" Antifa youngsters who definitely have not seen the world or studied the Gulag, are stupid enough to support a coup d'etat in the United States. Their leaders should be tried for treason.

Note that it is the British Anti-Fascist Action (AFA), a militant "anti-fascist" group founded in 1985, gave birth to the Antifa movement in the United States, as Gatestone Institute points out. It may be argued that the now "American Antifa" is a British invention.[cxlvi]

BLM recently decapitated and destroyed a statue of Colonel Hans Christian Heg, a Norwegian immigrant who spent his life fighting slavery before dying in battle leading Union soldiers in the Civil War.[cxlvii]

While tearing down statues of people such as Christian Heg, Black Lives Matter seem less and less about helping black lives, and more like useful idiots fulfilling globalist goals.

BLM and Antifa now strongly resemble the Islamist terror group ISIS that suddenly appeared out of nowhere in 2014. What about Africa and Egypt? Is BLM heading there to tear down monuments too, like ISIS did? The pyramids were built by slaves, there are mummies of ancient pharaos who owned slaves in African museums.

What about the African tribesmen who sold slaves to Arabs that they had taken from other black tribes when at war? This is how slavery began long before the white man was involved. Is the BLM going to demand that African tribes who owned slaves erase their history and change their names?

What about tearing down the legacy of African leaders who in history profited from the black slave trade? What about the Arabs who bought slaves from the black tribes? The white slave traders only waited at the coast as they were unable to enter the interior of Africa. Why no attacks on Arab nations?

What about Arabs who had white slaves?[cxlviii] After all, more whites brought as slaves to North Africa than blacks to US, writes Larry Elder.[cxlix] Is it only black slaves that matter?

As it was British Christian preachers and activists who in the British Empire ended black slavery, is BLM not going to celebrate the glory of the British?[cl] The British Empire should be hailed for its work to end slavery.

The politicized agenda of the Black Lives Matter seem more about fulfilling the Democrat goal of removing the democratically elected President. And yes, the donations to BLM apparently go straight into Act Blue[cli] which reportedly is a Democrat fundraiser that has given hundreds of millions to white, rich politicians.[clii]

The main point of all this being: This will likely be the very element that ends up reelecting Trump in November, 2020 if democracy and fair elections still stand in the United States, as sane American are likely to vote for law and order Trump more than ever.[cliii]

CHAPTER 13

Sad Riots Demonize Blacks and Help Trump's Reelection

The murder of George Floyd in Minnesota raised legitimate anger over police violence, but sadly has been heavily abused by infiltrating political and anarchist groups. As they intermingle with those rightfully protesting against racism, looting and civil unrest will be blamed on blacks. The riots may end up creating more division and segregation between races than ever before.

Donald Trump may be the sole benefactor in the upcoming election, as sane Americans will want law, order and jobs – not Democrat-supported defunding of police and an anarchy of rude, white millennials who think it is good fun to burn cars, smoke marijuana and quit school.

The irony, of course, turned out to be that George Floyd killed himself by a drug overdose, are we to believe the Medical Examiner's report and autopsy: No police officer killed him. He apparently died from a three times fatal overdose of Fentanyl Opioid. Both the official autopsy and the records from the police body camera show that Floyd was extremely high from drug use and consequently died of an overdose. This was first pointed out by Dr. Paul Craig Roberts on his famous blog that reaches millions.

Nowhere in the mainstream media is there any mention of Floyd's existing serious health conditions, his drug addiction, and the level of fentanyl in his blood. Why? Are we not interested in finding out the truth?[cliv]

The medical examiner's report has been ignored by the presstitute media and by public authorities including the prosecutor who indicted officer Chauvin, writes Dr. Paul Craig Roberts, a leading political economist and regular contributor to The Herland Report.[clv]

A small example of the politicized undertones: Why is the current debate on slavery solely focused on black slaves sold to white owners? It only discusses racism from whites toward blacks, not the other way around. All whites are evil now?

To insinuate this creates massive anger from the white population, as none of them was ever a slave owner. Watching how white Americans who never owned slaves kneel in front of black Americans who never were slaves, demonstrates how people don't think rationally.

As Confederate statues are torn down, one also wonders: Are we going to ask Egypt to change its name and tear down its African pyramids, which were built by slaves? And destroy mummies of pharaohs that had slaves? Isn't that exactly what we criticized ISIS for doing just a couple years back, smashing ancient irreplaceable statues?

Slavery began in Africa when the black tribes, in war with each other, sold the slaves they took from other tribes to the

Arab slave traders. No white man was around. The Arabs then transported the slaves to the coast. Are we going to change the names of African tribes too? And tear down the dignity of their names in history? What about Muslim leaders who had slaves?

White men who were unable to enter the harsh tropical environment in the interior of Africa waited with ships in the coastal regions for the Arabs who had bought slaves from other black tribes in the interior. Not only white men were involved in the black slave trade. African tribesmen and leaders, the Arabs *and* the white slave ship owners all bought and sold slaves.

In other words, everyone understands by now that there are forces at work that wants us all to hate each other. Many are so easily duped by feelings created by media propaganda and groupthink that they do not reflect upon how the race question now is being exploited to create even more hatred.

Antifa radical anarchists and white, young millennials with Black Lives Matter signs smash windows, loot and spray paint American cities with black American slogans. Who pays these youngsters?[clvi]

Civil unrest now unravels in the U.S., step by step according to the exact same Gene Sharp manual, even with bricks and stones administered to the raging demonstrators, just like what happened at Tahrir square in Egypt in 2010.[clvii]

What the Black Lives Matter movement does not sufficiently understand is that they are probably being used by billionaire white capitalists who aim to get to Trump.

Before Coronavirus, the U.S. under Trump saw the lowest unemployment rates among blacks in over 50 years, and prison reforms that benefit blacks were carried out by the Trump administration. Black Americans are front and center in his administration.

When the record low black unemployment rate was announced during the Trump annual State of the Union address, Democratic Speaker Nancy Pelosi even refused to clap, as we have seen.[clviii] It apparently was nothing to her. She even tore up the Trump speech on national television.

As we all remember, it was the Democrats that fought *for slavery*, supported the Confederate flag, joined the KKK and so on. The hypocrisy is baffling. The aim may be to end democracy in the United States, control Congress and taxpayers and assemble the power into the hands of the very few. And all of those are white and rich.

And yes, racism and the abuse of Afro-American youngsters to form a mob that will serve your own political agenda is evil. The misuse of the young minds of America, the focus on the color of someone's skin, the reverting to ethnic identities rather than national unity regardless of race produces horrible results. Who pushes for this return of the National Socialist focus on race? Who pushes for the end of the civil rights' movement in yet another age?

Racism simply is evil. A person cannot do anything about the color of his skin, whether he is white or black. By inciting that ethnic identity is the problem, we are doing the very same that Dr. Martin Luther King Jr. fought against.

The Baptist preacher and later martyr for his message of nonviolence and the end of segregation in America, Dr. King, wrote from the Birmingham jail letter horrid stories of institutionalized racism (selected parts): "We have waited for more than three hundred and forty years for our God-given and Constitutional rights. I guess it is easy for those who have never felt the stinging darts of segregation to say "wait." But when you have seen vicious mobs lynch your mothers and fathers at will and drown your sisters and brothers at whim; when you have seen hate-filled policemen curse, kick, brutalize, and even kill your black brothers and sisters with impunity; when you see the vast majority of your twenty million (the N word removed and substituted with Afro-American) brothers smothering in an airtight cage of poverty in the midst of an affluent society; when you suddenly find your tongue twisted and your speech stammering as you seek to explain to your six-year-old daughter why she cannot go to the public amusement park that has just been advertised on television, and see tears welling up in her little eyes when she is told that Funtown is closed to colored children, and see the depressing clouds of inferiority begin to form in her little mental sky, and see her begin to distort her little personality by unconsciously developing a bitterness toward white people; when you have to concoct an answer for a five-year-old son asking in agonizing pathos, "Daddy, why do white people treat colored people so mean?"; when you take a cross-country drive and find it necessary to sleep night after night in the uncomfortable corners of your automobile because no motel will accept you; when you are humiliated day in and day out by nagging signs reading "white" and "colored"; when your first name becomes "nigger" and your middle name becomes "boy" (however old you are)...There comes a time when the cup of endurance runs over and men are no longer willing to be plunged into an abyss of injustice where they experience the bleakness of corroding despair. I hope, sirs, you can understand our legitimate and unavoidable impatience."[clix]

CHAPTER 14

Riots Are Another Attempted Coup d'etat

When Gene Sharp first wrote the manual on how to create a revolution, in 1993, he probably did not expect that in 2020 his methods could be used in the attempt to overthrow a democratically elected U.S. President, Donald Trump.

The tactics of infiltrating legitimate movements for political purposes follows the Gene Sharp[clx] manual *From Dictatorship to Democracy*: Use a grievance the local population has against the system, identify and support those who oppose the current government, infiltrate and strengthen opposition movements, fund them with millions of dollars, organize protests that seem legitimate and have paid political instigators dress up in regular clothes to blend in.[clxi]

It happened in Maidan, Ukraine, leading to the overthrow of the government, where mercenaries later said they were instructed by Americans to begin shooting. This remains to be confirmed.[clxii] It happened in the George Soros-inspired "color revolutions," and in Serbia it led to the fall of Slobodan Milosevic. It happened in the Egypt "Arab Spring" and took down Hosni Mubarak. It happened in Libya with the killing of Moammar Gadhafi. It happened in Syria, as "peaceful protesters" suddenly were not that peaceful after all but turned out to be infiltrated by al-Qaida members.

Now it is happening in the United States, where civil unrest unravels step by step according to the exact same Gene Sharp manual, even with bricks delivered, just like the Tahrir Square in Egypt in 2010. It is as though the Arab Spring, Libya and Syria has come to the United States.

Twitter erupted with locals photographing the piles of bricks all across Texas, laid out along the path where demonstrations were to be held, and Instagram films showed young, white, black-clad girls smashing windows, writing Black Lives Matter on walls and being stopped by black women who asked them why they did this. "We are going to be blamed for this looting," said the young blacks to the white rioters.[clxiii]

A BBC documentary[clxiv] demonstrates the links between Gene Sharp's alleged CIA material[clxv] on how to overthrow governments, the CANVAS resistance in Serbia that led to the overthrow of the government and the Arab Spring revolutions.[clxvi] BBC credits Gene Sharp as the man behind the toppling of Mubarak in Egypt, Milosevic in Serbia and Viktor Yanukovych in Ukraine and the color revolutions.

In 2009, Egyptians dissatisfied with the Mubarak leadership in Egypt went to Belgrade, Serbia, to learn the Gene Sharp tactics that had worked so well there in overthrowing Milosevic.[clxvii] The new method of professionalizing mass protests as a method to overthrow governments proved very successful in the Arab Spring.[clxviii] Journeyman even did a documentary on the massive Gene Sharp CANVAS success.[clxix]

WikiLeaks showed how the U.S. Clinton administration helped the protesters; James O'Brien, the Clinton administration's special envoy to the Balkans even explained its success. Foreign Policy: "Revolutions are often seen as spontaneous. It looks like people just went into the street.

But it's the result of months or years of preparation. It is very boring until you reach a certain point, where you can organize mass demonstrations or strikes. If it is carefully planned, by the time they start, everything is over in a matter of weeks."[clxx]

The murder of George Floyd seems abused by infiltrating political groups that intermingle with those rightfully protesting against racism, and cause looting and civil unrest they know will be blamed on blacks.

The rightful grievance over racism is being used now to oust Trump since Russiagate, impeachment, the Coronavirus scandal and other attempts have not worked. The aim is to end democracy in the United States, control Congress and politics and assemble the power into the hands of the very few.

On the topic of Russiagate: Are we nothing but conmen, eager to lie and defame one another, publicly displaying to the rest of the world the lack of national responsibility and accountability that permeates the current American establishment?

As it turned out by the examinations of Special Council, Robert Mueller, the Russiagate and Russian collusion story was not provable, yet the mainstream media willingly spread into all the corners of the world.[clxxi]

While it is true that foreign states' spying activity probably never has been greater, stories that are pushed by the media should contain some level of truth. Next, the Democrats' massive impeachment of President Trump also failed.

The sum of the mess in the recent years makes America look both treacherous and deceitful for all the nations to see. It is such a shame that we are no longer known for honorability and justice, a demonstration of the current cultural decay. When something like this can be done to a President, what level of justice can ordinary citizens expect?

Judicial Watch' President, Tom Fitton has called Russiagate a Deep State coup attempt, an ongoing mutiny against the people's choice for President in the United States. Sen. Rand Paul demanded the investigation of the Obama aides who pushed the Russiagate conspiracy hoax to the public.[clxxii]

Those responsible for spreading the hoax should be held accountable, defaming America's democratically elected top official and tainting the nation's reputation all across the globe. In case anybody wonders, we look like idiots to the Russians, for failure to stop this embarrassing story.

Even before this new nail in the coffin of the notorious mainstream media, 77 % of the American public believed that the media do not speak the truth.[clxxiii] Russiagate goes down in history as a remarkable display of American stupidity.

To return to the Black Lives Matter movement, which arguably is being used in the same power scheme: What its ideological leaders do not understand is that they are being used by the billionaire white capitalists who are fighting to push the working class even lower and end the national sovereignty principles President Trump stands for in America.

It is all about who will own the United States and have free access to its revenues: either the American people under democracy, or globalist billionaires. The rise of totalitarianism as socialists merge with capitalist interests to create state control in America is baffling to watch.

CHAPTER 15

Marxist Socialism Provides Strict Control

As drug abuse, social upheaval and lack of national unity engulf the United States, many ask where things went wrong. Some argue that this is the end result of the 1960s Neo-Marxist social revolution that completely redefined Western values and thereby caused fundamental division and cultural decline. I argue this point in *New Left Tyranny. The Authoritarian destruction of Our Way of Life.*[clxxiv]

The radical drug loving hippies that started off protesting later became the ruling class, the professors at the universities, the chief editors at the publishing houses and the media. Gullible, young millennials have now spent years listening to their teachings and all joined Antifa, believing that the enemy of state is the Christian values that founded the American Constitution.

They believe that atheist anarchy, destruction of private property and civil war paves the way for peace and racial harmony. Probably not knowing it, these young minds are being exploited by cunning men, much in the same manner as the politicized masses in the Arab Spring. As we know, the

Arab Spring led to war and civil war in country after country with millions displaced in the Middle East.

The transnational globalist business model works perfectly with socialism as its leaders make sure that the people give up all their private rights and then assemble all the national wealth into state systems. The globalist robbery capitalism then pays the politician lavishly, and he funnels billions of state funding – taxpayers' money – into whatever the globalist wishes for.

Historically, Marxism fought for an internationalist structure, a system that worked across borders. The same is the aim for the globalist capitalist system which depends on borderless societies, its owners not paying taxes to any nation, outsourcing jobs to where the requirement for worker's payment is low.

Many do not reflect on the simple fact that the large capitalist owners supported Nazism and greatly profited from working alongside National *Socialist* Hitler in manufacturing consent in Germany. After the war, socialism was implemented in Europe as the welfare state rose to power. In *New Left Tyranny*, I have argued that the EU represents a regional socialism much in the same way as Germany pre-war implemented National *Socialism*. In both systems, the capitalist owners worked hand in hand with the socialist politicians.

What Marxists often forget, probably since socialism seems to be a religion to them, is that the Capitalist model is not an ideology. It is an economic model. Capitalists don't care at all about ideology, they care about profit and economic gains. With Karl Marx as the Marxists' God, they are stuck in their wish for utopia, working to achieve future goals, while the Capitalist works to accomplish profits in the here and now.

This means that to a Capitalist who hopes to maximize profit, it does not matter whether he works with Marxists, Socialists, or fellow Capitalist – whether Chinese, Japanese or people from Albania. He is as likely to support China against his own president as anything else. Profit sways him. Ask Joe Biden, as recently pointed out by President Trump as he compared a Biden win with a China win in the US elections, 2020.

CHAPTER 16

Will Neo-Marxism Finally Cancel America?

It may be argued that the socialists' brilliance is pretending to be for the worker, while gathering the power into the hands of a state elite who controls the economy. It is key to attain control over the population and no ideology does it better than socialism.

One may say that freedom becomes, in a socialist system, the right to agree with the Marxist elite. The rebel journalist and author, Karl Marx' detested religion, traditional values, historical Western ideals and its bourgeoisie. When reading him, the question becomes: Did Karl Marx really aim to help the working class in a proletariat class struggle, or was the idea simply to replace one ruling class with a new ruling elite – the Marxist tyrants?

Many questions arise when examining Marxism and its off springs such as socialism, Communism, National Socialism (NAZI), neo-Marxism and so on. When looking at the Marxists' brutal, bloody revolutions, the economic decline in the nations that implemented socialism, Marx' intention may be questioned.

Was Karl Marx' intention actually to help the proletariat or the working class, or did he simply wish for the Marxist class - his own friends – to take the power from the bourgeoisie and become the new feudal, Marxist lords?

Are the Communist class struggle speeches only that propagate the propaganda narrative which lures the working class into believing that the socialists will fight for them? All the while, the "people" are only being used as a "useful mob" designed to be led in the direction its Marxist rulers design, in the power game of ruthless politics?

It may be argued that no people have been as subdued, deprived and controlled as the people in socialist and Communist states. To this day, several decades after the Berlin wall fell in 1989, the Communist Eastern block countries are still far behind the nations that chose capitalism and allowed more freedom for its people and ownership over their own income. Even though the market capitalist system has its clear drawbacks, it still represents the best among the worst systems available.

If Marx intention was for the socialist class to take over the power, with in reality little regard for the working class, his socialism is the perfect tool for the next generation robbery capitalism capitalists.

Marx does, in that case, not fight for the class struggle for the working class, but rather the power structure for the Marxist elite take-over. And this is exactly what has happened, as the working class in the West are being robbed from their wealth as the globalist system outsources jobs to China and the East.

The 1960's student rebellion was clearly Neo-Marxist, its leaders such as Herbert Marcuse used the term about his ideology. Marxism found its revitalized shape after World War II in the Frankfurt School in Germany. I address this in *New Left Tyranny* as well.

This was an intellectual group connected to the Institut für Sozialforschung (Institute of Social Research) in Frankfurt am Main. They agreed on a fundamental philosophical approach deriving from Marxism.

Philosophers such as Theodor W. Adorno (1865-1952), Herbert Marcuse (1898-1979), Friedrich Pollock (1894-1970) and Max Horkheimer (1895-1973) launched the concept of "critical theory," implying that science should change conditions in social structures in order to push society in the direction of the neo-Marxist world view.

The pre-war *socialist* ideology continued even after National *Socialism* lost in Germany, only slightly modified. The intellectuals of the Frankfurt School remained Marxist, looking for ways to moderate the Marxist pre-war ideology in order to make it more applicable to a post-war situation. At the time, they felt that both Communism and National Socialism had come off on the wrong track, yet they did not denounce its Marxist roots.

In the 1950s, as the word New Left emerged, the Neo-Marxists sought to distance themselves from the Marxist authoritarian traits yet ended up perfecting the lack of tolerance for plurality in the 1960s hippie movement.

In the 1960s, the New Left came full circle in completing Karl Marx's objective in *The Communist Manifesto* from 1848, namely to "melt the solid into air." Marx' hatred of traditional religion, traditional politics and institutions made him a radical revolutionary Jew who spent his life defining radical socialism.

Marx is famous for "the class struggle", but did he really aim to help the working class? He introduced a system in which no real changes were made: Marx basically suggested for the state to take over the role of the feudal lords and the worker remained as deprived of the ownership to his revenues as ever. And who were to rule the state? His own, new ruling elite: The Marxists.

This is the secret of socialism that hardly anyone reflects on: Its aim was never to give the power to the working class, but to implement a new state elite that would rule the workers, control the taxpayer's money and state revenues? The Marxists simply desired to take the power away from the hereditary, aristocratic ruling class.

Marx' gospel of envy is at the heart of Marxism. The hereditary class was to be replaced by a new ruling Marxist class. The hated "factory owner" was replaced by a Marxist factory owner, thus perfecting the class struggle of envy.

The new ruling class would, after killing off the old in a bloody revolution as seen in the 1917 Russian revolution, take power and form a strong state. While pretending to be the saviors of the worker, the Marxist class was to become the new "state lords."

This was to be done with brutal force and terror. Social evolution only takes place through the systematic destruction of the old system, it was said. "There is only one way to shorten and ease the convulsions of the old society and the bloody birth pangs of the new – revolutionary terror," Marx famously stated.

Marx' ability to motivate his followers to become the new tyrants is remarkable. Marxism certainly has not given the power to the people, but rather concentrated it in the hands of the very few. This is why modern socialism goes perfectly hand in hand with the globalist robbery capitalism, devoid of the Protestant ethic. In such a system, nobody cares about the working class.

CHAPTER 17

Donald Trump for Nobel Peace Prize

Simply by actively attempting to pull US forces out of Syria,[clxxv] the work to end the North Korean crisis, the efforts to end the Kashmir crisis and the persistent push to solve the Israel-Palestinian issue, President Donald Trump is a far more worthy Nobel Peace Prize winner than Obama ever was.[clxxvi]

If any time was the right to award the Peace Prize, it would be when Arab nations, such as the United Arab Emirates and Saudi Arabia acknowledge the existence of the state of Israel.

Jews have been a part of the multicultural and multi-religious Middle East for thousands of years. To deny Jews their rightful place in their region of inheritance simply speaks for the deep-rooted level of anti-Semitism that sadly permeates the environment.

Just as Christianity was a Middle Eastern religion long before the Islamic conquests, both Christians, practicing Judaic Jews and other religions such as the Bahai are natural parts of the Middle Eastern fabric of diversity. Donald Trump respects this and has done great work attempting to raise the bar of respect for diversity in the region.

And where exactly do the Gaza billions in aid go? Hardly anybody in the West asks the question. We all remember very well how Yasser Arafat died a billionaire. The estimated international aid controlled by Arafat amounted to around USD 5.5 billion since 1994, and he seems to have overseen all disbursements, according to Forbes.[clxxvii]

It sure did not go to the streets of Gaza or Jericho – evident to everyone who has visited the area. No hospitals built, no schools, hardly any roads, houses not rebuilt after Israeli strikes. The money seems to have evaporated into thin air.

Hardly anyone disagrees in that Obama did not deserve the Peace Prize. It was probably given to him as a reward for being the first Afro-American President in the United States, yet awarding according to the race card clearly as the blue sky has never been a requirement from Alfred Nobel, the founder of the prize.

Obama received the Nobel in the midst of escalating the war in Afghanistan, days after taking office, having proved nothing as regard to his actions deserving the honor. The Obama award became an embarrassing scandal and a strong signal that the Norwegian Nobel Committee is politically rigged, tied to the Democrat cabal. To repeat, Obama had done nothing - zero - to fulfill the Alfred Nobel requirements for the Prize.

The Norwegian Nobel Committee has become notorious for almost solely giving the prize to the Liberal US media favorites, disregarding the will of Alfred Nobel.

In Sweden, Alfred Nobel's family are rattling the sables in discontentment of the rampant politization in the hands of the Norwegians, the claim being that the Committee willfully disregards Nobel's will and awards the prize to human rights activists, climate activists and others.[clxxviii] The Committee is also criticized for misusing it as a political tool to influence countries' domestic policies.[clxxix] Nobel's family openly suggest that the prize should be returned to Sweden.[clxxx]

The Alfred Nobel will clearly states that the Peace Prize is to be, "annually awarded to the person who shall have done the most or the best work for fraternity between nations and the abolition or reduction of standing armies and the formation and spreading of peace congresses...advocates of peace, have conferred the greatest benefit on mankind, the most worthy shall receive the prize."[clxxxi]

Family member and professor, Michael Nobel especially criticized the award given to the Chinese, Liu Xiaobo in 2010. He stated: "Alfred Nobel's will from 1895 clearly states that the prize was to go to peace-makers, defined as persons who worked to prevent wars through fraternity, that is through global work for the disarmament of nations based on global justice and institutions.

Still, the Nobel Committee has the past ten years on purpose disregarded Nobel's will and chosen Prize winners from their own preferences. Human rights activists, climate activists and a long list of others have been given the prize, even if their work does not lay within Alfred Nobel's specific vision of peace bringing, as stated in his will."[clxxxii]

Dr. Daniel W. Drezner wrote an ironic open letter to the Nobel Committee in The Washington Post, yet insinuating what so many speak about, that the Norwegian system is rigged.[clxxxiii] Trump is fully aware of the politization and tweeted: “I think I’m going to get a Nobel Peace Prize for a lot of things, if they gave it out fairly, which they don’t.”[clxxxiv]

I assert that Donald Trump is by far the worthiest candidate to the Nobel Peace Prize 2019. President Trump was a notable peacemaker in the North Korea crisis which implied nuclear threats and succeeded in averting an escalation; his repeated effort to halt the Syria war and now pull out has led to avoiding an all-out World War.

His work to end the relentless neo-con aggression on Russia is highly admirable as we now are all post Russia Gate which turned out to be such a hoax that shamed America.[clxxxv] Or an attempted coup, as director of investigations at Judicial Watch, Chris W. Farrell, asserted in a Herland Report TV show to be found on the Herland Report YouTube channel.[clxxxvi]

But will Trump ever get the prize in the current climate where the Norwegian Committee has leaders that hardly can speak English, with members broadly lacking international experience, stuck in their provincial Oslo bubble where the only respected view to have is the regressive neo-Marxist illiberal Left? [clxxxvii]

I say this as a Norwegian conservative with long experience in participating in the media: The Norwegian press is completely and utterly submerged in an outdated neo-Marxist Leftwing propaganda to a degree that reminds us more of the Soviet Union. It may be argued that its elite are so controlled and blind to reality that they don't even understand it themselves.

Or even worse, they do understand that the applied socialist strategy of propaganda coercion forces the population into silence in such a way that hardly anyone dare speak their mind. This affects the politicians in a most dramatic way, as the media mob may attack and tear to shreds the reputation of anyone protesting. It is all but democratic and all but a system that respects the will of the poor people that suffer under brutal neo-Marxist repression.

Seemingly totally sold to the narrative of the owners of CNN and *New York Times*, the Norwegian Committee has the past years become no more than an extended wing of the endless war, American neo-con movement. It is a shocking scandal. The Prize goes rather to 15-year olds from Bangladesh or the forests of Congo rather than to world leaders who have averted world wars.

I would assume Greta Thunberg, the 16 year old media puppet[clxxxviii] pushed by billionaires to "end divestment in oil" and create a world energy shortage" which we might assume they later will profit from.[clxxxix]

Thunberg is now publicly subjected to child abuse with no objections from her parents. Again, Dr. Drezner who might have been ironic, but yet was straight to the point: "I hope you stupid Europeans can read good English and accept this nomination and act fast to award President Trump the Nobel."

CHAPTER 18

Bishop Harry Jackson and Racial Healing

At The Herland Report YouTube channel, we regularly have the privilege of sit downs with leading intellectuals, bestselling authors and activists.[cxc] In a divisive time, the wisdom of the forefront spiritual leader,[cxci] Bishop Harry Jackson, in the Herland Report exclusive interview below, gives Christian perspectives to the current hatred and ethnic conflict in America.[cxcii]

Bishop Harry Jackson has been featured in the leading media outlets and is a frequent guest at the Donald Trump White House. He is senior pastor at Hope Christian Church in Maryland, educated at Harvard Business School, the founder of the High Impact Leadership Coalition and a co-founder of The Reconciled Church initiative: Healing the Racial Divide Movement – an effort to heal the racial division first in the church and then the nation.

The bishop says in this exclusive interview, which shocked me as it gave insight into topics that I was not aware of to that extent before: "America has always had racism fueled by fear and pride beneath the surface. There was a time when a man with my skin color looking at a beautiful white woman would only have to raise my voice and say 'you're cute,' and I would be tortured and lynched on the spot. That is the America that existed in the '30s, '40s and the '50s."

The bishop says: "My sense of fighting for justice in this generation was born out of my very first years of life. My father was on his way home from a voter registration event, and he was stopped by a state trooper in the state of Florida, not far from Florida University."

"The state trooper made him kneel and took out his weapon and put it right next to his ear and pulled the trigger, temporarily deafening my dad. Then he said, using the 'N-word': 'If you do anything like that again, next time I'll kill you!' By the time he came home, he decided that he was going to leave the South as soon as he graduated. So, there was this sense that there was a deep injustice in the country."

"I will never forget me being 12 years old sitting down with my dad in the kitchen of our home in Avondale, Cincinnati.[cxciii] He began to tell me that he felt that racism was an emotional and mental disease, and he said some of the people who helped him most in his life had been white, and some who had done the most reprehensible to our family had been black. He said that I shouldn't judge people by their skin color. This was before Dr. King's statements became so famous."

It is peculiar to watch how Marxist movements such as Black Lives Matter are not lifting up martyr Dr. Martin Luther King Jr. Under his leadership, the peaceful movement succeeded in ending the legal segregation for Afro-Americans in the South and across the United States.[cxciv] He was awarded the Nobel Peace Prize in 1964. Why do Black Lives Matter not like the Martin Luther King message? Is it because he was a Baptist Christian preacher who advocated for non-violence and for all to love one another?[cxcv] Is it because he was a Christian?

In the Letter from the Birmingham jail where he was imprisoned for participating in a nonviolent demonstration against segregation, Dr. King writes his Christian proclamation: "Just as the eighth-century prophets left their little villages and carried their "thus saith the Lord" far beyond the boundaries of their hometowns; and just as the Apostle Paul left his little village of Tarsus and carried the gospel of Jesus Christ to practically every hamlet and city of the Greco-Roman world, I too am compelled to carry the gospel of freedom beyond my particular hometown. Like Paul, I must constantly respond to the Macedonian call for aid."

And Dr. King does not hide the gross racism in America: "In any nonviolent campaign there are four basic steps: Collection of the facts to determine whether injustices are alive, negotiation, self-purification, and direct action. We have gone through all of these steps in Birmingham. There can be no gainsaying of the fact that racial injustice engulfs this community. Birmingham is probably the most thoroughly segregated city in the United States."

"Its ugly record of police brutality is known in every section of this country. Its unjust treatment of (the N word translated to Afro-Americans) in the courts is a notorious reality. There have been more unsolved bombings of Afro-American homes and churches in Birmingham than in any other city in this nation. These are the hard, brutal, and unbelievable facts. On the basis of them, Afro-American leaders sought to negotiate with the city fathers. But the political leaders consistently refused to engage in good-faith negotiation."[cxcvi]

Bishop Jackson comments on this: "Back in the civil rights days, Martin Luther King Jr. was esteemed by most Americans as an iconic classic American, and if you go past him, you have got to go all the way back to the revolutionary days to have people that seemed to embody 'Americanism'. Martin Luther King put his case to the American public by lifting up the Constitution in his left hand and a Bible in his right hand. Meaning, depending on which group he spoke with, he had to have a higher framework, a way of referencing truth and righteousness. I believe America is losing her ability to call the nation back to accountability, because we no longer really honor the Constitution or the Bible at the level that we once did."

Bishop Jackson points out: "I believe that my biblical way put me in the conservative side of the camp, politically, back in the early 2000s. On the other hand, we do find that black conservatives and white conservatives have two different worldviews, meaning that they look through different lenses at the world."

"We talk about righteousness and justice, and blacks often look through the justice lens because we have been discriminated against in America. Then, very often, white evangelicals often look through the righteousness lens. But, the Bible doesn't teach righteousness and justice separately, they are to be intertwined, together and one unit."

Asked about the current divisiveness in America, he replies: "Even Jesus prophesied about this. He said that ethnic groups were going to rise up in a carnal and perhaps even demonic inspired sense of superiority. Jesus said in the last days that nations would revolt against nations; and the underlying Greek word for this is *ethnos*."

"I would report to you that the division that you are seeing now has been here in America for 400 years. I see the traces of tribalism as a valid explanatory model to understand the United States. I prefer to say it like this, rather than to use the word 'racism.' The Bible teaches us that we are one race. But tribalism in Africa, for example, means that people who look alike, at least to me, still kill each other. Here, I would say tribalism and generational poverty/class is a high driver that trump the impact of race in the United States."

"In other words, if I am raising a family that in four generations has not been able to get out of the ghetto or have any higher education, the chances of poverty are significantly higher, no matter what kind of atonement would be given. Imagine the America that has endured generational poverty, lack of education and exposure, you then have a massive class distinction. You're locked into a world with less opportunity and then on top of it all, you're black. That describes part of the problem."

About Christianity, the bishop says: "I believe that by standing with God and obeying the rules of God, if you will, creating an atmosphere of justice for the less fortunate and those who can't cry out for themselves, God is glorified. I believe we are in a time in which God himself is exposing

America and saying this is where we really are. I want to say that racism is not only a white man's problem. We have black racists who are talking about taking up arms."

"The great apostle John says that 'we know that we've passed from death unto life because we love the brethren.' In John's days, that meant people of Middle Eastern descent, Roman descent, African descent. So, if you do not have love for the brethren and cultivate that love for the people that don't look like you, we have a counterfeit Christianity."

CHAPTER 19

The "Black and White" Polarization

The U.S. assassination of Major General Qassem Soleimani has illustrated quite well how little many in the West know about the realities on the ground in the various Middle Eastern countries.[cxcvii] The killing was instantly politicized domestically by Democrats, as if yet another reason to "remove Trump" in the ongoing attempted coup d'eat against the nation's elected President.[cxcviii]

Remarkably ignorant Hollywood stars and the Democratic left reacted as though the military leader, head of Iranian covert operations and militia groups, were some kind of "peace dove" on endless diplomatic missions.[cxcix]

It seems to us Europeans that many in the United States live behind Soviet walls in their utter ignorant perception of the international world. The Herland Report recently spoke to Virginia State Senator, Richard Black on this topic.[cc] Hollywood actress Rose McGowan's serves as an example: "Dear #Iran. The USA has disrespected your country, your flag, your people. 52% of us humbly apologize. We want peace with your nation. We are being held hostage by a terrorist regime. We do not know how to escape. Please do not kill us. #Soleimani."[cci]

McGowan, who states in her Twitter account that "I am here to make society better" actually says the United States is "being held hostage by a terrorist regime" when President Trump is the people's elected President. She thereby openly states that she does not respect the outcome of democratic elections.[ccii]

When a President is duly and constitutionally elected by the people in the nation, McGowan thinks that makes it a "terrorist regime"? The stupidity is unbelievable. The Hollywood actresses who praise the Iranian system would not even be allowed to land in Tehran without putting on total Islamic veils and covering even the slightest part of her hair, arms, legs and so on.

Let them try to start demanding "free speech" in Iran, for example, and the building of Christian churches, for that matter. McGowan is but one example of the same phenomenon engulfing the West:

We have this chronic tendency to categorize reality into either "good" or "bad" nations or politicians. Some countries are considered "good," others "evil regimes," corresponding to the geopolitical quest for territorial dominion.

The left, whose "benevolent billionaires" own the U.S. media, do all in their power to demonize Trump. Anything Trump does is "evil," regardless of what the President says or does. Anything Hillary Clinton says, on the other hand, is "great, just and should be listened to." Had it been "the good"

Obama sending off drones and killing Middle Easterners, chances are he would receive the Norwegian Nobel Peace Prize for it.[cciii]

We get it. The idea is that the world is divided between "good" and "evil" – "Trump is evil" and "Iran is paradise on earth." Israel is "evil" too.[cciv] "All Jews are bad," and "all Iranians are good"? The degree of anti-Semitism today is unbelievable.[ccv]

The childish, Disney-like portrayal of nations or politicians, idealized in a "black and white" setting, is extremely dangerous. It does not correspond to reality and sends its believers into a world of utopianism.

The categorization technique serves yet another purpose – maybe the most important: It gives a nation an outer enemy, something "evil to fight." Iran serves this purpose to Israel, and Israel to Iran.

Iran is particularly clever in the game of demonization. Anyone who knows this massive country is fully aware of its religious priesthood's clever usage of the fear of outer enemies to quench diverging domestic opinions. When you incite fear into a nation, its people are easily subdued into submission under their political rulers.

And how is it with free speech in Russia, by the way? Russia Today (RT) is remarkably great at criticizing the West and America, and equally very clever in avoiding criticism of Russia, their own President or their own power structures. If you have noticed, RT seems more and more to be about bashing *only* the West. What about reporting critically what happens in Russia? That seems not to be on their agenda.

Don't get me wrong: Russia is a wonderful place with a great history and people, Iran equally a great nation with such a rich history, not to forget the wonderful Iranian food. But that does not make these nations the saints of the world while President Trump "is always the devil." Power corrupts, regardless of race or culture. There is corruption everywhere, not only in Washington.

What we need is more unbiased knowledge about other nations, grounded, in reality, not progressive utopianism. Let us get realism rather than idealism and a balanced view on what is going on in the world.

CHAPTER 20

Anti-White America and the Hatred of the Male

The Liberal neo-Marxist obsession with race – the idiotic notion that being right or wrong corresponds to a person's skin color – is now overflooding the Democrat party and its socialist disciples. It has been efficiently tried out in South Africa with tragic consequences.

Ever since Marxist ANC took over with Western help, racism against so-called "white citizens" has exploded in the country.[ccvi] Sadly, the Identity Politics' narrative, which stems from the misguided Liberal progressivism in the 1960s, now makes us speak about "black" versus "white" again, a conversation which often ends up accentuating the color-awareness, which is the precise element that classical Western values wished to eradicate.

The historic Christian value, the belief that all humans are equal, regardless of race, creed or class, is one of the founding elements in Western civilization. Since the 1960s, these ideals have steadily been diminished in the new, atheist West.

Identity Politics tends to assume that when people of darker skin color react, they are always right and should be applauded, while individuals of whiter skin colors always are the perpetrators. Thus, if injustice in the past is to be levelled, the white man should be blamed for everything that went wrong.

Ever since this doctrine was implemented in South Africa, hundreds of thousands of whites have left the country, emigrating to New Zealand, Mosambique, South America and other destinations.[ccvii]

As President Cyril Ramaphosa opened up for amending the Constitution for land expropriation without compensation[ccviii] from white South Africans, he effectively made it legal for black people to steal the land of farmers with impunity.

White South Africans have been in Africa since as early as the 1500s, and are now forcefully removed as their property rights are withdrawn. Many blacks are openly calling for "the killing of whites". The media, following the Identity Politics' narrative, hardly reports on the issue.[ccix]

Marxist ANC is following in the footsteps of Robert Mugabe,[ccx] the notorious President of Zimbabwe who also forced the highly skilled white farmers out of his country, with the detrimental effect of the economy collapsing, as black farmers without the skills on how to run large scale agricultural projects took over.

The media reactions following Covington Catholic High incident in Washington DC in January 2019,[ccxi] is an excellent example of the same failed progressive narrative in America. The Covington scandal may be one of the worst demonstrations of racism against whites in the US in a long time. The mainstream media automatically judged that "the white, heterosexual, Christian boys, wearing MAGA hats" were to blame, and did not even bother to check the facts. According to the media, the white skin color seems to be all the evidence needed to attack.

Dr. Paul Craig Roberts, one of the leading political economists in the USA and a former editor of the Wall Street Journal, recently pointed out in a Herland Report TV interview, that Identity Politics, which the Liberals so passionately embrace, has appointed new exploiter group to be the "white heterosexual males."[ccxii]

This group is completely defenseless and not protected by any quotas, prohibitions against hate speech or hate crimes. You can say anything about a white heterosexual male, Roberts states, but you can't say the slightest thing about blacks, homosexuals, Hispanics or women. whole notion of class conflict has been replaced by gender, race and sexual preference conflict.

In the Covington scandal, the media, having ticked off all the boxes for sub-groups in society that currently have no protection whatsoever, – white, male, Christian, Trump supporter – Twitter rants read all kinds of threats and violent suggestions that wished the Catholic boys dead, bombed, their school destroyed and so on.

We welcome the letters from Covington Nick Sandmann's lawyers, preparing for defamation lawsuits. The video about the boys version of the story, corroborated with video clips from the scene tells it all.[ccxiii] Here is the hypocrisy from the broadly "white mainstream media": No national mobster attack on the group of four black Hebrew Israelites' who, as may be heard in the video, abused both the white boys, the native Americans and others who happened to pass by.

The native Americans were addressed in a remarkably rude and racist way. Why the full-frontal attack on the white Catholics who offended nobody - only smiled - and no mention of the ugly language from the Black Hebrew Israelites? We suspect the American progressive mainstream press would never dare to create the same type of national lynching mode against the black Hebrew Israelites as they did with the young white boys. Note that racism is judging someone based on his skin color alone.

As it even turns out, the native American Indian who wore the drum, is reportedly known to be a notorious liar. The man was never a Vietnam veteran, although this has been his claim in media reports. Is he protected from criticism due to his skin color and identity as a native?

The traditional, Western principle of equality regardless of race, creed, ethnic background definitely seems to be a lost principle in America. Yet, it must be noted that the Nick Sandmann defamation did not end so well for the mainstream media. His lawyers sued and the assault on the young Catholic, Christian boy was so horrible that CNN and Washington Post[ccxiv] alone have so far paid Sandmann[ccxv] around 500 million USD in damages.[ccxvi]

Trump and the West as the New Soviet Union

CHAPTER 21

The Christian Martin Luther King Jr. Values

Understandably enough, it is not always easy for the population to comprehend what is going on behind the media smokescreen. For example, when President Trump walked across Pennsylvania Avenue from the White House to inspect the damages from riots at the historic St. John's Episcopal Church in June, 2020. As he was photographed holding a Bible in his right hand, the mainstream media could not stop mocking his choice to hold onto that Bible.[ccxvii]

Without mentioning that the "peaceful protests" had strongly damaged the historic site, the media avoided telling the whole story. But why did Trump hold up the Bible and why did he pledge to bring "law and order" to a nation in anarchy?[ccxviii] Why does a man in modern America, facing the organized revolt that seems to come from the very enemies he made when stating "America first" years ago? Which values clash in the current Marxist revolution in the United States?

Let me remind everyone of the massive impact that Christianity and the revolutionary message of Jesus Christ has had on the Western civilization. As we live in an age of atheist intolerance, where the mainstream media constantly focus negatively on Christians, we need to remember how groundbreaking the Christian faith really is.

Over 80 % among Americans[ccxix] state that they "believe in God", research showing that only 2.4 % of the world population are atheists[ccxx] – according to Pew Research Forum, Encyclopedia Britannica, ISSP 2008 and so on.[ccxxi] There are remarkably few atheists, really. The masses believe in God and do their prayers. So, why are atheists and religion mockers allowed to control the mainstream narrative and with bullying tactics relentlessly work to belittle the Christian values that once made us great?

Several of our most important values come precisely from the Judeo-Christianity heritage and its ethics. I have spoken about this at length in my book *New Left Tyranny. The Authoritarian destruction of Our Way of Life.*

Let me repeat some of its points here, as it is vital to comprehend why Christian values are important. Professor at Yale and Harvard, historian Robert R. Palmer and Joel Colton state in *A History of the Modern World* that Christian philosophy defined the concept that humanity is inclusive of all people. This represented a new view on the value of human life and was truly revolutionary.[ccxxii]

When you look at the early Christians, they are remarkably engaged in social work among the lower classes, the poor, the widows and the fatherless. This attitude of caring for those who are deprived of benefits in life, is at the center of Christian thought. Jesus was born in a manger, far from the palaces of the rich. One of the founding values in Christianity is humility and the requirement to love one another, regardless of class, creed and gender.

The French philosopher Bernard-Henri Levy and atheist Michel Houellebecq have pointed out that we would not have had human rights without the Jewish-Christian incredibly bold idea about the sanctity of man. Created in the likeness of God, man becomes a highly valuable as a created being.[ccxxiii]

The famous professor, Palmer states that it is simply impossible to exaggerate the importance of Christianity's influence on Western values. Without Christianity, we would probably not have had the principle of equality, which unleashed the revolutionary idea that each man, regardless of class, gender, and race, has a unique value.

Later this view was understood as a secular idea, but its religious origin is a historical fact. German philosopher and atheist, Jürgen Habermas states in *The Dialectics of Secularization: On Reason and Religion* that Christian theology in the Middle Ages and Spanish scholasticism as the origins of what we today call human rights.[ccxxiv]

Habermas also says that secular moral political theory has made a grave mistake in excluding Christian ethics, as these have in history demonstrated its ability to motivate individuals to do good. Somehow, Christianity has been able to motivate the individuals that together compose our society to care more for one another.

After more or less abolishing Christianity from the public discourse – which has been done in Europe for decades – this collective ability for solidarity seems to wane. Egoism takes its place, hedonism with personal pleasure as its value, materialistic gains become forefront.

Former Pope Benedict XVI says that the focus on scientific and technological progress has produced a society that now lacks empathy.[ccxxv] This is the greatest threat. Without solidarity, individuals become destructive towards one another. Even democracy depends on citizen solidarity or else it easily becomes the tyranny of the mob.

These were the values that the Christian preacher and civil rights' icon, Martin Luther King Jr. fought and was martyred for. In the Birmingham jail letter, he writes: "But as I continued to think about the matter, I gradually gained a bit of satisfaction from being considered an extremist. Was not Jesus an extremist in love?—"Love your enemies, bless them that curse you, pray for them that despitefully use you." Was not Amos an extremist for justice?—"Let justice roll down like waters and righteousness like a mighty stream."

"Was not Paul an extremist for the gospel of Jesus Christ?—"I bear in my body the marks of the Lord Jesus." Was not Martin Luther an extremist?—"Here I stand; I can do no other so help me God." Was not John Bunyan an extremist?—"I will stay in jail to the end of my days before I make a mockery of my conscience." Was not Abraham Lincoln an extremist?—"This nation cannot survive half slave and half free." Was not Thomas Jefferson an extremist?—"We hold these truths to be self-evident, that all men are created equal." So the question is not whether we will be extremist, but what kind of extremists we will be. Will we be extremists for hate, or will we be extremists for love? Will we be extremists for the preservation of injustice, or will we be extremists for the cause of justice?"[ccxxvi]

What becomes apparent is the neo-Marxist demonization of Christianity itself. Many simply do not understand how important the Christian message and moral requirement to love one another was for the forming of central Western ideals. The Christian concept of equality transcends class, race and gender.

The example of the Eastern philosopher and son of Mary, Jesus even tells the stories about how he spoke and engaged with people from all walks of life: Jews, Samaritans who were detested by Jews, Roman military officials who were hated by the locals, he engaged with women in a radically free manner that shocked his followers. His simple message was "love God and one another." Everything about him was radically implementing a new way of disregarding class, gender and status. Again, he was even born in a manger, in a stable, in order to make the point.

This is the mystery of which the Eastern Orthodox Church speaks: "God cannot be grasped by the mind. If he could be grasped, he would not be God," as Evagrius of Pontus writes.[ccxxvii]

The philosophical idea and roadmap to inner peace as defined in Christianity is: "Be honest, honorable, honest, accountable, faithful. Keep the commandments and get a great life that prepares you for the afterlife, in which there will be a judgment on how you spent your short-lived days on this planet."

As with any philosophy or ideology, it is not about what you say, but what you do. Many a religious person has the most horrid values practiced, yet happy to stand in church on a Sunday and pretend like nothing is wrong. It is how you live that matters, not the fake "Christian talk". In the Gospel of John, Jesus is cited as angered by people who came to him, saying "Lord," and asked them "Why do you call me Lord, but refuse to do as I say?"

Arguably, some of the very worst evil people are "Christians" and thereby blasphemers of God in using his name, while refusing to walk the talk. Some are relentlessly citing the holy books and scriptures, but equally remarkably far from living according to its recipe.

The immensely serious question of Christian hypocrisy again brings us back to the Christian preacher and martyr, Dr. Martin Luther King Jr. who led the civil Rights Movement in the 1950s and 60s, and his analysis on the white moderate who does not stand up against injustice: "I must confess that over the last few years I have been gravely disappointed with the white moderate. I have almost reached the regrettable conclusion that the (N...word is changed to Afro-American)'s great stumbling block in the stride toward freedom is not the White Citizens Councillor or the Ku Klux Klanner but the white moderate who is more devoted to order than to justice; who prefers a negative peace which is the absence of tension to a positive peace which is the presence of justice."

"We will have to repent in this generation not merely for the vitriolic words and actions of the bad people but for the appalling silence of the good people. We must come to see that human progress never rolls in on wheels of inevitability. It comes through the tireless efforts and persistent work of men willing to be coworkers with God, and without this hard work time itself becomes an ally of the forces of social stagnation."[ccxxviii]

Dr. Martin Luther King Jr. chose the nonviolent kind. In the Birmingham jail letter, he writes: "You may well ask, "Why direct action, why sit-ins, marches, and so forth? Isn't negotiation a better path?" You are exactly right in your call for negotiation. Indeed, this is the purpose of direct action. Nonviolent direct action seeks to create such a crisis and establish such creative tension that a community that has consistently refused to negotiate is forced to confront the issue. It seeks so to dramatize the issue that it can no longer be ignored. I just referred to the creation of tension as a part of the work of the nonviolent resister."

He adds: "I have earnestly worked and preached against violent tension, but there is a type of constructive nonviolent tension that is necessary for growth. Just as Socrates felt that it was necessary to create a tension in the mind so that individuals could rise from the bondage of myths and half-truths to the unfettered realm of creative analysis and objective appraisal, we must see the need of having nonviolent gadflies to create the kind of tension in society that will help men to rise from the dark depths of prejudice and racism to the majestic heights of understanding and brotherhood." [ccxxix]

Even Karl Marx took his message from a Christian pool of thought, as socialism is inherently focusing on the rights of the lower classes. The idealized dignity of the worker, the willingness to fight for the rights of the common man and those with lower income not to be degraded by rich landowners, clearly reflect Christian attitudes. Respect for all, regardless of rank is a genuine Christian idea.

CHAPTER 22

Authoritarian Social Media Giants

The historic, Western definition of tolerance signifies respect for disagreement. Wildly diverging opinions mark a tolerant debate where all the pieces of information are discussed. High tempers, loud voices, yet intelligent arguments based on rationality and relevance to the topic. Freedom of speech implies maximum tolerance for a variety of viewpoints.

But *not* among the modern-day Liberal Left. They seem to detest freedom and love the totalitarian clampdown on free speech. The state is to control us all and free speech is only for those who agree with the Leftwing gospel of hedonism and social cohesion. As political columnist and senior editor at The Stream, Rachel Alexander, put it in World Net Daily, the largest Conservative online news network in the United States:" Liberals are gradually censoring out conservative speech through political correctness because they know if conservative speech continues to get through, it will convince more people not to be leftists.

They portray conservative speech in the most offensive way possible to scare people from identifying as conservatives.

All the words that apply to themselves – racist, sexist, bigoted – they transfer to conservatives in order to deflect from their own prejudicial views."[ccxxx]

The mainstream media has reflected this kind of illiberal and intolerant bigotry for years. Yet, for a brief moment some hoped for social media freedom in the West. When facing mainstream censorship, one could, at least online, discuss perspectives of truth that are taboo and omitted from the politicized Western public discourse.

But especially the past year we have seen disturbing totalitarian signs from giants such as Facebook, that seem bent on growth to such a degree that they are willing to compromise on liberty and justice. First, the allegation of Russian meddling, then violating the privacy act and leaking personal information of tens of millions. The company's stocks plummeting, millions deleting their accounts.[ccxxxi]

For some reason, Facebook now thinks that the remedy to mistrust is to add the exact same kind of totalitarian censorship that everyone dislikes so much in the press. The aim is apparently to lose even more of its former fans. The past year we have seen what many believe to be the clamping down on Christians, Muslims, conservatives, anti-war activists and those critical of Islam in the West.

When under the pretext of de-platforming hate speech, one ends up removing "those voices that Liberals do not like," we are close to completely shutting down free speech in social media. Facebook joins the mainstream media as the non-trusted.[ccxxxii]

A recent survey showed that two thirds of Americans and almost 80 % among the British[ccxxxiii] do not believe that the media speaks the truth.[ccxxxiv] Maybe not strange, considering revelation after revelation of dishonesty. For example, CNN, collaborating with known Al-Qaida officials or the undercover tapings of a CNN producer saying that CNN knew well that the Russiagate story[ccxxxv] was a phony, but only used it to get good ratings.[ccxxxvi]

Another CNN producer notoriously stated that the " American voters are stupid as **it."[ccxxxvii] Needless to say, these attitudes display a remarkably dishonest and unethical attitudes with remarkably low respect for democracy, that seem to permeate the CNN structures. Whether the stories are true or not does not matter much, as long as it gives CNN good ratings?

The Facebook era is over, says Gina Bianchini, CEO at Mighty Networks.[ccxxxviii] Facebook's monopolistic network with 2.2 billion users who innocently thought sharing pictures and private information was fun are now slowly realizing the increasing Liberal politization. Not to mention the sneaky algorithms attempt to control your behaviour.

As Facebook figured out how to make money on the platform, the increasing amount of algorithms began clogging up the simplicity that we all loved. Facebook was the alternative to mainstream Liberal terror, now they are a part of precisely that which we hate.

And the one million attempts to make you "boost a post" or "speak to one of our business managers," terrorizing your email inbox with "business proposals" and hindering your attempts to talk to friends. Finally, you turn to private messaging platforms to avoid the Facebook noise and regain the freedom in life.

Silicon Valley guru, Jaron Lanier's talk with Channel 4 is worth watching.[ccxxxix] He warns against the world of algorithms and speaks about how the massive control that you are not aware of in social media is ruining your life. Symptomatically enough, when a post about the Facebook critic Jaron Lanier interview was posted on my Facebook it was censored as "against community standards". Maybe we'll take Lanier's advice and shut down social media and get back to email newsletters, podcasts and our favourite websites.[ccxl]

CHAPTER 23

Dr. Ron Paul About the Internet Cartel

The movement toward Orwellian censorship in various online platforms such as Amazon, Facebook, Twitter and Google seems to steadily gain momentum. As over 90 percent of the media in America is owned by the very few ultra-rich companies, it has never been easier to push propaganda and manufacture consent. Now the internet free-speech arena seems to be shutting down too in a historic display of illiberal intolerance toward specific groups in the West.

The allegation is that the anti-globalist, conservative and religious groups are particularly targeted, those who voice the need to respect national sovereignty and international law. This sends a strong signal to the population: If you voice concern and protest, you might be jailed or removed from Facebook and Google.

In Europe, the culture of fear is rampant, people think twice before they voice an opinion, like in the old Stasi systems of East Germany. People expect to be shut down any minute, and carefully take the time to save pictures and valuable conversations from social media. Trust in Facebook and Google seems to diminish by the hour, many expecting the free speech to soon be over on the internet.

In the recent abortion debate in Catholic Ireland, that changed the "no to abortion" 8th amendment of the constitution, the anti-abortion campaign groups were reportedly banned from using Facebook and Google.[ccxli] While pro-abortion groups, allegedly funded by George Soros, were favorably pushed all over the mainstream media,[ccxlii] the no-side received almost zero positive media coverage or coverage at all.[ccxliii]

This all creates a sad feeling that we are slowly slipping into totalitarianism, which Hannah Arendt so eloquently described in "The Origins of Totalitarianism." She showed how individual liberty suffocates in a democracy when peer pressure and a culture of consensus takes over and the masses are controlled by the state.

She points out that a totalitarian government then becomes even worse than a dictatorship, pushing for total control of what the citizens think about the family, religion, politics and so on.

The founder of The Liberty Report, Dr. Ron Paul, one of America's most respected voices, recently gave an exclusive interview[ccxliv] to The Herland Report where we spoke about the issues concerning the growing intolerance in the West.[ccxlv] Dr. Paul is world famous for his critical views of the Federal Reserve, the military-industrial complex, NSA surveillance and U.S. participation in the wars abroad.[ccxlvi]

As censorship seems to be the new fashion in illiberal America, Dr. Paul surprisingly says that the trend will eventually die out in much the same manner as the Soviet Union. The system will come to an end: "The collapse of the Soviet system happened because it was a failed system. I think we have a failed system now that's affecting our culture.[ccxlvii]

That is why you have the cultural Marxists in our universities preaching. They want to disrupt our culture so that they can mold it back together in a different type of centralized control. It is cultural more than economic Marxism. And certainly, the introduction to the neoconservatives has been a big deal."

In the interview, posted on YouTube, Dr. Paul adds: "The Soviet system dod not develop anything, and the same is happening to us right now. The only thing that we export now are dollars. We get a good deal because we have managed, through our military and economic power, to maintain a dollar system. Therefore, we have a tremendous advantage, but it's a system that is deteriorating, and it must be reversed."

He also says: "The people who are on the defensive now are the people who believe in the superpower state. Even the neoconservatives are on the defensive because everything they do fails. Look at the Middle East. All our policies are failing. We help our enemies as much as we are supposed to help our allies."

In *The Origins of Totalitarian Democracy*, T. J. Talmon notoriously states that totalitarian democracies break with the originally liberal form of democracy and are characterized by an unusually low respect for the right of the citizen to individual freedom.

Because the goal of politics becomes that citizens should obediently agree with the mainstream media narrative and express themselves in socialist groups, peer pressure becomes the method to gain and retain control of citizen behavior.

CHAPTER 24

Martin Luther King Jr. and the Totalitarian State

In times of massive political upheaval such as what we are now witnessing, the German philosopher Hannah Arendt who lived to see World War II and the totalitarian Nazi regime up close is worth remembering. She wrote *The Origins of Totalitarianism* in which she discussed how it was possible for a democratic state such as Germany to turn into a cold blooded totalitarian state. Wasn't modernism supposed to bring us closer to freedom for all? Instead the modern, atheist world has brought upon us more atrocities and Gulags than we all thought possible.[ccxlviii]

Arendt makes the point that a totalitarian system may become even worse than dictatorships, as the latter implements fear of death when speaking up against the authorities, but totalitarian states does the same, but in a more subtle way.

The aim in totalitarian systems is to control every aspect of a person's life, his views on the family, genders, his feelings towards the church, religion – every aspect of life is to be controlled. In such states, the population is held in fear of repercussions from the police and state authorities, in constant fear of losing their jobs, their reputation, their friends. Fear becomes the tool to keep the population in check. Nobody dares to say much, out of trepidation for what may happen then.

One of Arendt's main points was that precisely because modern democracies incorporates well developed institutions and the hierarchical structure, people tend to obey orders without daring to think freely. They view themselves as part of a system with little or no personal responsibility.

Again, Dr. Martin Luther King Jr.: If the laws are just, this is no problem. But if the laws are unjust and represent a violation against certain minorities or the majority, while others are given the right to forcefully step on "the little man", the laws become a problem. The legal system then becomes a problem, because it institutionalizes injustice.

The distinction between laws that provide more freedom and justice and laws that ensure state censorship and fear, is of immanent importance. The value system in a society – its moral codex –is key. Does our moral codex, be it the neo-Marxist or traditional Conservative or any in between, provide more justice to all? Or less justice between groups? Does it provide more respect for plurality or less? Does it respect differences of opinion or not? What about diversity, are we allowed to be different and think differently? Does the moral codex motivate individuals for solidarity and empathy? Does it provide wealth to its citizens or only to the elites? Can a wealthy individual buy its politicians? Will the justice system treat the widow and the fatherless the same way it treats its millionaires when appearing in court? All these questions become vital.

Arendt found that it was not the desire to be brutal to certain ethnic groups such as Jews and Gypsies, that was the root cause for the "obedience towards the state" that permeated the German society. It was the indifference, lack of empathy and willingness to obey status quo that permeated the German population. Since group think was vital in this society, no one dared to step out of the group. Those who did, quickly ended up in the same concentration camps where intellectual dissidents joined the Jews and others who were unwanted.

The point is that societies that cultivate just laws prosper. Societies that allow the corruption of political powers, the rise of the few to own everything, the right of the few to pay and "buy" politicians, the gross neglect of certain subgroups in society to rot in ghettos for decades, the lack of public health systems, sufficiently good public schools, the lack of respect for law and order, the disdain for the moral codex that establishes right and wrong, the corruption of institutions so that the rich can pay his way to freedom, the lack of good leaders who care for the well-being of the population – these unjust societies do not prosper.

To quote America's great Christian prophet and martyr, Martin Luther King Jr.: "You (the authorities) express a great deal of anxiety over our willingness to break laws. This is certainly a legitimate concern.

One may well ask, "How can you advocate breaking some laws and obeying others?" The answer is found in the fact that there are two types of laws: there are just laws, and there are unjust laws. I would agree with St. Augustine that "An unjust law is no law at all."

"Now, what is the difference between the two? How does one determine when a law is just or unjust? A just law is a man-made code that squares with the moral law, or the law of God. An unjust law is a code that is out of harmony with the moral law."

"To put it in the terms of St. Thomas Aquinas, an unjust law is a human law that is not rooted in eternal and natural law. Any law that uplifts human personality is just. Any law that degrades human personality is unjust. All segregation statutes are unjust because segregation distorts the soul and damages the personality."

"We can never forget that everything Hitler did in Germany was "legal" and everything the Hungarian freedom fighters did in Hungary was "illegal." It was "illegal" to aid and comfort a Jew in Hitler's Germany. But I am sure that if I had lived in Germany during that time, I would have aided and comforted my Jewish brothers even though it was illegal. If I lived in a Communist country today where certain principles dear to the Christian faith are suppressed, I believe I would openly advocate disobeying these anti-religious laws."

Dr. Martin Luther King Jr. adds:" There was a time when the church was very powerful. It was during that period that the early Christians rejoiced when they were deemed worthy to suffer for what they believed. In those days the church was not merely a thermometer that recorded the ideas and principles of popular opinion; it was the thermostat that transformed the mores of society."

"Wherever the early Christians entered a town the power structure got disturbed and immediately sought to convict them for being "disturbers of the peace" and "outside agitators." But they went on with the conviction that they were "a colony of heaven" and had to obey God rather than man. They were small in number but big in commitment. They were too God-intoxicated to be "astronomically intimidated." They brought an end to such ancient evils as infanticide and gladiatorial contest." [ccxlix]

So, let us return to the faith of Dr. Martin Luther King Jr. and install again the belief in a just society. As President Trump explicitly states, he aims to restore the respect for traditional, Western values and make America great again. I shall end where I began: Donald Trump may be the most demonized President in US history, simply because his enemies own the media and the established globalist elite.

With his "America First" slogan, he launched a massive attack on the globalist billionaire's empire that for decades has benefitted from the outsourcing to jobs and wealth to China and the ultra-rich.

Trump seeks to reinstate the national sovereignty of the United States, return jobs to the working class and rebuild America. Will he succeed or will we face the end of the West as we know it?

Endnotes

[i] https://www.businessinsider.com.au/these-6-corporations-control-90-of-the-media-in-america-2012-6

[ii] https://www.marketwatch.com/story/just-62-people-own-as-much-wealth-as-half-the-worlds-population-oxfam-2016-01-18

[iii] https://www.hannenabintuherland.com/usa/corona-is-good-news-and-produces-mass-wealth-for-the-richest/ and https://www.hannenabintuherland.com/usa/billionaires-fortunes-skyrocket-since-covid-19-corona-pandemic-began-no-more-democracy/

[iv] https://www.forbes.com/sites/katevinton/2016/06/01/these-15-billionaires-own-americas-news-media-companies/#15b2c93a660a

[v] https://www.who.int/news-room/detail/14-12-2017-up-to-650-000-people-die-of-respiratory-diseases-linked-to-seasonal-flu-each-year

[vi] https://www.who.int/mediacentre/news/statements/2017/flu/en/

[vii] https://edition.cnn.com/2018/09/26/health/flu-deaths-2017--2018-cdc-bn/index.html

[viii] https://www.worldometers.info/coronavirus/country/china/

[ix] https://www.hannenabintuherland.com/europa/china-is-smarter-than-the-west-will-gain-post-corona-scandal-hanne-nabintu/

[x] http://www.xinhuanet.com/2020-02/20/c_1125603476.htm

[xi] https://www.businessinsider.com/5-million-left-wuhan-before-coronavirus-quarantine-2020-1?amp;IR=T&r=US&IR=T

[xii] https://www.cna.com.tw/news/acn/202003140249.aspx

[xiii] https://www.hannenabintuherland.com/europa/how-china-and-the-media-caused-market-crash-by-selling-us-fear/

[xiv] https://www.nejm.org/doi/full/10.1056/NEJMp2003762#article_references

[xv] https://www.hannenabintuherland.com/europa/who-leader-tedros-a-ghebreyesus-is-chinas-man-to-push-west-to-destroy-itself-corona/

[xvi] https://www.hannenabintuherland.com/usa/western-billionaire-control-of-democracies-bill-gates-covid-19/

[xvii] https://edition.cnn.com/2020/04/13/world/cnn-coronavirus-coverage/index.html

[xviii] https://lidblog.com/dr-tedros-adhanom/?__cf_chl_captcha_tk__=6630df5457bb27e86546a7ecf-1c37348091ede63-1598961041-0-AYv2miwqPPwb22N-

fxA_SIlFoaX_sgCUXaHWXFEqaW44EgF0S3ueY1DL-
RGN3Av8GV22odgdz6ZJ5iEjto-SIXHwbP4TTZXeEjtp-
CnnQmyt0kByejxKtqRob9DaK5wb5kSqkVOmNfQQN-
QCCsL9PtgxxIw8abHEEyfqOYxXp8G85eGYE8bjX-
irOqQ7M-oqg7RrECK7NFPLinIuQIfl-nY1qlf_8bnz-
MTPjn8x6fL-24t00eZnfYmQni997JHWoNu-XTsz6g-
Z4I24Y_60moMHgEsVgrAzN59hDn0hpKOm-
rvWxalUGRSP6yvMV7c7chMg9kZa_XdRsHNEd0VylWl-
NqjydsJ4n-GuwqBsFftNTPwsWJ0IpGZxs2LLAkJpnxVB-
kAErF9IflJXxC0G8ZQpD-CePkg1Pt8yYZO2GNbHzer-
w1zG77s207uBYKciOT4D5vpuHApU73Aglfjxm0fZhI-
ASfx8roTP1rBE5RtJQdz5KfhttOREaZ77d_JCnqHDsl-
NUCx8-kw

[xix] https://euobserver.com/coronavirus/147699

[xx] https://www.dailywire.com/news/leading-swedish-epidemiologist-slams-british-scientist-whose-paper-triggered-worldwide-lockdowns-normally-quite-arrogant

[xxi] https://www.hannenabintuherland.com/financial-crisis/imperial-report-who-horror-scenarios-questioned-among-allegations-of-politization/

[xxii] https://www.youtube.com/watch?v=bfN2JWifL-CY&t=764s

[xxiii] https://unherd.com/thepost/giesecke-stands-firm-swedish-death-rate-will-go-down/

[xxiv] https://www.who.int/emergencies/diseases/strategic-and-technical-advisory-group-for-infectious-hazards/members/biographies/en/index2.html

[xxv] https://www.youtube.com/watch?time_contin-
ue=212&v=d6MZy-2fcBw&feature=emb_logo

[xxvi] https://www.youtube.com/watch?v=PC3nptwY-
50I&feature=emb_logo

[xxvii] https://www.hannenabintuherland.com/europa/
dr-bhakdi-extreme-measures-violate-human-rights-pre-
vents-herd-immunity/

[xxviii] https://www.youtube.com/watch?v=JBB9bA-gXL4

[xxix] https://www.hannenabintuherland.com/financialcri-
sis/3-million-go-hungry-in-the-uk-today-due-to-lock-
down-policy-richisunak/

[xxx] https://www.hannenabintuherland.com/europa/coro-
na-panic-shuts-down-economy-biggest-loss-yet-to-come-
hanne-nabintu/

[xxxi] https://www.hannenabintuherland.com/usa/the-feder-
al-reserve-cartel-the-eight-families-who-own-usa-dean-
henderson-herlandreport/

[xxxii] https://finance.yahoo.com/news/russia-won-t-
blink-first-220000234.html?guccounter=1&guce_refer-
rer=aHR0cHM6Ly93d3cud25kLmNvbS8yMDIwLzA-
zL2dsb2JhbGlzdHMtY2hpbmEtbWVkaWEtc2VsbGluZy-
11cy1mZWFyLw&guce_referrer_sig=AQAAAIdNNy-
O9pvlEVpAMkcurvtGDNBD3jpOQzBwdGSe60c7-WaZI-
O6T4DTHgZOsTJUET9kXPNsvgGYMWN6YUQ6NheyX-
MXuhr_JwR4gtCKxMGQoCEi5o0Rd_1pfLoKDmgIxF-
WzXTyb8xW_XE0OgGaWyw124U0ALJ2m3fz4mwcI_
BG1ebJ

xxxiii https://www.hannenabintuherland.com/europa/corona-panic-shuts-down-economy-biggest-loss-yet-to-come-hanne-nabintu/

[xxxiv] https://www.hannenabintuherland.com/usa/amid-market-crash-cnn-admits-trump-had-massive-economic-gain/

[xxxv] https://www.hannenabintuherland.com/mideast/corona-causes-china-to-rise-as-west-helplessly-battle-meltdown/

[xxxvi] https://www.msn.com/en-us/news/world/republicans-it-s-time-to-ban-the-chinese-government-from-twitter-for-its-whitewash-of-coronavirus-history/ar-BB11ycQE?ocid=spartanntp

[xxxvii] https://www.globalresearch.ca/china-locked-hybrid-war-us/5706687

[xxxviii] https://www.cnbc.com/2020/01/15/trump-and-china-sign-phase-one-trade-agreement.html

[xxxix] https://www.hannenabintuherland.com/usa/amid-market-crash-cnn-admits-trump-had-massive-economic-gain/

[xl] https://www.hannenabintuherland.com/interviews/breaking-senator-richard-black-on-deep-state-military-complex-endless-wars/

[xli] https://www.sciencedirect.com/science/article/pii/S1201971219303285

[xlii] https://steigan.no/2020/03/koronavirus-situasjonsrapport-fra-italia/

[xliii] https://www.timesofisrael.com/israeli-virologist-urges-world-leaders-to-calm-public-slams-unnecessary-panic/?fbclid=IwAR39XpQKP19c4_VQzf4DXWPRKDPEll6g-kjJGG7z5mZ4aT3ZZUYGvSd7JDJU

[xliv] https://www.youtube.com/watch?v=aerq4byr7ps&feature=youtu.be

[xlv] https://edition.cnn.com/2020/03/13/uk/uk-coronavirus-response-boris-johnson-intl-gbr/index.html

[xlvi] https://www.hannenabintuherland.com/europa/how-china-and-the-media-caused-market-crash-by-selling-us-fear/

[xlvii] https://www.hannenabintuherland.com/europa/who-leader-tedros-a-ghebreyesus-is-chinas-man-to-push-west-to-destroy-itself-corona/

[xlviii] https://twitter.com/billgates/status/1243418437163995137?lang=en

[xlix] https://cepi.net/wp-content/uploads/2020/04/CEPI_2019-Board-of-Directors-Report-and-Annual-Accounts_incl.-Auditors-Report_final-website-WS_compressed.pdf

[l] https://www.politico.eu/article/bill-gates-who-most-powerful-doctor/

[li] https://childrenshealthdefense.org/news/government-corruption/gates-globalist-vaccine-agenda-a-win-win-for-pharma-and-mandatory-vaccination/

[lii] https://www.msn.com/en-us/news/other/a-potential-coronavirus-vaccine-funded-by-bill-gates-is-set-to-begin-testing-in-people-with-the-first-patient-expected-to-get-it-today/ar-BB12e01f

[liii] https://www.zerohedge.com/geopolitical/did-bill-gates-just-reveal-real-reason-behind-lock-downs

[liv] https://www.youtube.com/watch?v=Xe8fIjxi-coo#t=34m14s

[lv] https://www.health.com/condition/cold-flu-sinus/how-many-people-die-of-the-flu-every-year

[lvi] https://www.worldometers.info/

[lvii] https://www.hannenabintuherland.com/usa/corona-death-counts-not-necessarily-correct-hospitals-list-covid-19-as-cause-of-death-based-on-assumption/

[lviii] https://patriot-fire.net/2020/03/30/dr-fauci-covid-19-may-turn-out-to-be-like-a-bad-flu-season/

[lix] https://www.youtube.com/watch?v=lGC5sGdz4kg&feature=emb_logo

[lx] https://www.dailywire.com/news/epidemiologist-warns-of-unintended-consequences-from-lockdowns?utm_source=facebook&utm_medium=social&utm_campaign=benshapiro&fbclid=IwAR1EQOzTiFIMsPPYR-ONRIiLsum7i5ECNl8bCGI9BF-Q25scXy9B0q6vgOKo

[lxi] https://www.youtube.com/watch?v=JBB9bA-gXL4

[lxii] https://off-guardian.org/2020/04/01/could-the-covid19-response-be-more-deadly-than-the-virus/

[lxiii] https://www.washingtontimes.com/news/2020/apr/28/
coronavirus-shutdown-skeptics-challenge-establishm/

[lxiv] https://www.rystadenergy.com/globalassets/pdfs/rys-
tad-energy_covid-19-report_29-april_2020_public-ver-
sion.pdf

[lxv] https://www.washingtontimes.com/topics/new-york-
city/

[lxvi] https://www.youtube.com/watch?v=bfN2JWifL-
CY&t=764s

[lxvii] https://twitter.com/NikolovScience/sta-
tus/1248252848183201792

[lxviii] https://www.worldometers.info/

[lxix] https://edition.cnn.com/2020/04/13/world/cnn-coro-
navirus-coverage/index.html

[lxx] https://www.hannenabintuherland.com/financialcri-
sis/3-million-go-hungry-in-the-uk-today-due-to-lock-
down-policy-richisunak/

[lxxi] https://www.youtube.com/watch?v=pzA69MZHPhU

[lxxii] https://www.foxnews.com/opinion/gutfeld-on-net-
works-fact-checking-trumps-address

[lxxiii] https://www.businessinsider.com/opi-
um-and-heroin-production-in-afghanistan-has-in-
creased-2016-10?r=US&IR=T

lxxiv https://blogs.wsj.com/economics/2016/02/09/immigrants-push-down-wages-for-low-income-workers-but-how-much/

lxxv https://www.npr.org/2016/12/22/506347254/latinos-will-never-vote-for-a-republican-and-other-myths-about-hispanics-from-20

lxxvi https://www.cbsnews.com/news/meet-the-mexican-americans-who-agree-with-donald-trump-on-immigration/

lxxvii https://www.nber.org/reporter/fall99/borjas.html

lxxviii https://eu.usatoday.com/story/news/politics/elections/2016/2016/11/09/hispanic-vote-election-2016-donald-trump-hillary-clinton/93540772/

lxxix https://www.cbsnews.com/news/meet-the-mexican-americans-who-agree-with-donald-trump-on-immigration/

lxxx https://nationaleconomicseditorial.com/2017/05/06/illegal-immigration-hurts-economy-depresses-wages/

lxxxi https://www.rollingstone.com/politics/politics-news/trump-takes-credit-obama-border-wall-818671/

lxxxii https://eu.usatoday.com/story/news/fact-check/2020/08/26/fact-check-obama-administration-built-migrant-cages-meme-true/3413683001/

lxxxiii https://www.hannenabintuherland.com/news/globalist-media-wants-to-stop-national-security-trump-speech/

lxxxiv https://drugabuse.com/featured/drug-trafficking-across-borders/

[lxxxv] http://www.nbcnews.com/id/33433955/ns/us_news-crime_and_courts/t/illegal-drugs-flow-over-under-us-border/#.XFCkuvZ2u8A

[lxxxvi] https://www.washingtonexaminer.com/report-nearly-all-998-of-illegal-drugs-shipped-to-us-from-mexico

[lxxxvii] https://www.foxnews.com/us/mexican-official-cartels-send-64b-in-drugs-into-us-annually

[lxxxviii] https://en.wikipedia.org/wiki/Syria%E2%80%93Turkey_barrier

[lxxxix] https://www.spiegel.de/consent-a-?targetUrl=https%3A%2F%2Fwww.spiegel.de%2Finternational%2Fworld%2Ffiring-at-refugees-eu-money-helped-fortify-turkey-s-border-a-1199667.html

[xc] https://www.hrw.org/news/2018/03/22/turkey-mass-deportations-syrians

[xci] https://www.spiegel.de/consent-a-?targetUrl=https%3A%2F%2Fwww.spiegel.de%2Finternational%2Fworld%2Ffiring-at-refugees-eu-money-helped-fortify-turkey-s-border-a-1199667.html

[xcii] https://eic.network/

[xciii] https://theblacksea.eu/stories/billions-for-borders/no-way-out/

[xciv] http://www.iamawake.co/the-eu-funded-wall-that-nobody-wants-to-talk-about-turkey-syria/

[xcv] https://www.thedailybeast.com/hungarian-nightmare-viktor-orbans-war-on-george-soros-3

[xcvi] https://ec.europa.eu/commission/presscorner/detail/en/MEMO_16_963

[xcvii] https://www.spiegel.de/international/world/firing-at-refugees-eu-money-helped-fortify-turkey-s-border-a-1199667.html

[xcviii] https://blogs.wsj.com/economics/2016/02/09/immigrants-push-down-wages-for-low-income-workers-but-how-much/

[xcix] https://www.oxfam.org/en/press-releases/62-people-own-same-half-world-reveals-oxfam-davos-report

[c] https://www.youtube.com/watch?v=EzBYxqtJSqc

[ci] https://cis.org/sites/default/files/2018-08/Jeh-Johnson-Cross-Border-Movement-of-Special-Interest-Alie...%20%284%29.pdf

[cii] https://www.meforum.org/57569/trump-and-the-gop-were-hardly-the-first?utm_source=Middle+East+-Forum&utm_campaign=91198757af-EMAIL_CAMPAIGN_2019_01_10_11_52_COPY_01&utm_medium=email&utm_term=0_086cfd423c-91198757af-33583797

[ciii] https://www.youtube.com/watch?v=hKpMO-5Jdx-s&t=2s&list=PLlrCpcbN8MxjcppbagnHfPKx8Rw-gEHbX4&index=3

[civ] https://www.youtube.com/watch?v=Xb1xHhGJjJk&feature=youtu.be

[cv] https://www.washingtonpost.com/politics/pelosi-shreds-trumps-speech-reflecting-a-tu-

multuous-year-in-washington/2020/02/04/c378856c-4771-11ea-ab15-b5df3261b710_story.html?hpid=hp_hp-top-table-high_pelosi-1145pm%3Ahomepage%2Fstory-ans

[cvi] https://www.washingtonpost.com/politics/2020/02/04/trump-exits-impeachment-apparently-unscathed-his-poll-numbers-reach-highs/

[cvii] https://www.washingtonpost.com/politics/2020/02/05/d2db682a-476d-11ea-ab15-b5df3261b710_story.html?hpid=hp_hp-top-table-high_debrief-1225am%3Ahomepage%2Fstory-ans&itid=hp_hp-top-table-high_debrief-1225am%3Ahomepage%2Fstory-ans

[cviii] https://www.hannenabintuherland.com/usa/impeachment-shock-listen-to-how-nancy-pelosi-explains-how-democrats-smear-and-lie/

[cix] https://www.foxnews.com/politics/pelosi-san-francisco-hair-salon-owner-calls-it-slap-in-the-face

[cx] https://gofossilfree.org/top-200/

[cxi] https://www.wnd.com/2019/09/greta-thunberg-show-public-child-abuse/

[cxii] https://www.hannenabintuherland.com/usa/bill-gates-on-climatechange-gretathunberg-push-for-divestment-in-oil-it-is-madness/

[cxiii] https://scottamyx.com/2019/03/18/interview-with-ingmar-rentzhog-the-founder-of-we-dont-have-time/

[cxiv] https://sverigesradio.se/sida/artikel.aspx?artikel=7127615

[cxv] https://www.washingtontimes.com/news/2015/aug/11/climate-change-industry-now-15-trillion-global-bus/

[cxvi] https://www.heritage.org/environment/commentary/follow-the-climate-change-money

[cxvii] https://buyingbias.org/2017/04/13/eco-groups-join-climate-march/

[cxviii] https://investingnews.com/daily/resource-investing/industrial-metals-investing/coal-investing/george-soros-coal-investing-climate-change/

[cxix] https://dailycaller.com/2018/02/19/george-soros-fossil-fuel-investments/

[cxx] https://buyingbias.org/2017/04/13/eco-groups-join-climate-march/

[cxxi] https://www.newsbusters.org/blogs/nb/mike-ciandella/2014/08/26/soros-clones-5-liberal-mega-donors-nearly-dangerous-george-soros

[cxxii] https://www.gurufocus.com/guru/george+soros/current-portfolio/portfolio

[cxxiii] https://climatechangedispatch.com/climate-hypocrite-george-soros-bets-big-on-fossil-fuels/

[cxxiv] https://oilprice.com/Energy/Crude-Oil/The-Struggle-Continues-For-Bankrupt-Shale-Drillers.html

[cxxv] https://www.wsj.com/articles/oil-and-gas-bankruptcies-grow-as-investors-lose-appetite-for-shale-11567157401

[cxxvi] https://www.ft.com/content/187f8176-f4f4-11e9-b018-3ef8794b17c6

[cxxvii] https://www.hannenabintuherland.com/usa/the-federal-reserve-cartel-the-eight-families-who-own-usa-dean-henderson-herlandreport/

[cxxviii] https://www.npr.org/sections/goatsandsoda/2016/08/19/490679863/the-little-boy-in-aleppo-can-one-photo-end-a-war

[cxxix] https://www.thedailybeast.com/greta-thunberg-is-the-climate-heroine-we-need

[cxxx] https://www.dailywire.com/news/51183/greta-thunberg-sailed-new-york-avoid-contributing-ashe-schow

[cxxxi] https://www.dailywire.com/news/52122/greta-snaps-we-are-beginning-mass-extinction-how-ryan-saavedra

[cxxxii] https://www.washingtontimes.com/news/2015/aug/11/climate-change-industry-now-15-trillion-global-bus/

[cxxxiii] https://www.youtube.com/watch?time_continue=117&v=eICiLRykTFg

[cxxxiv] https://www.npr.org/sections/goatsandsoda/2016/08/19/490679863/the-little-boy-in-aleppo-can-one-photo-end-a-war

[cxxxv] https://www.youtube.com/watch?v=PJOzBRy7dWs

[cxxxvi] https://letterfromjail.com/

[cxxxvii] https://www.hannenabintuherland.com/usa/collective-us-stupidity-threaten-to-demolish-national-unity/

[cxxxviii] https://disrn.com/news/video-surfaces-of-black-lives-matter-founder-saying-were-trained-marxists

[cxxxix] https://www.washingtonexaminer.com/news/black-lives-matter-co-founder-says-groups-goal-is-to-get-trump-out?fbclid=IwAR0Icb1x7xNhcrQrahzbcI8kxWX-zZ8E0LyMJhOgtFNCGfbGpR4303o_wu2U

[cxl] https://www.washingtonexaminer.com/news/black-lives-matter-co-founder-says-groups-goal-is-to-get-trump-out?fbclid=IwAR0Icb1x7xNhcrQrahzbcI8kxWX-zZ8E0LyMJhOgtFNCGfbGpR4303o_wu2U

[cxli] https://www.hannenabintuherland.com/usa/communist-antifa-red-army-faction-use-brutal-force-to-implement-anarchy-and-new-world-order/

[cxlii] https://www.marketwatch.com/story/for-millennials-socialism-and-communism-are-hot-capitalism-is-not-2019-10-28

[cxliii] https://www.hannenabintuherland.com/europa/repressive-new-left-authoritarian-marcuse-quench-majority-views-persecution-wnd/

[cxliv] https://www.amazon.com/CULTURE-WAR-Greatness-Weakened-Within/dp/1945757639/ref=sr_1_1?dchild=1&keywords=the+culture+war+hanne+nabintu+herland&qid=1598972728&sr=8-1

[cxlv] https://www.marketwatch.com/story/for-millennials-socialism-and-communism-are-hot-capitalism-is-not-2019-10-28

[cxlvi] https://www.gatestoneinstitute.org/16104/antifa-history

[cxlvii] https://wkow.com/2020/06/23/protesters-pull-down-forward-statue-outside-state-capitol/

[cxlviii] https://www.hannenabintuherland.com/usa/white-slavery-was-normal-in-the-bysantine-period-raymond-ibrahim-herland-report/

[cxlix] https://www.hannenabintuherland.com/usa/larry-elder-more-whites-brought-as-slaves-to-north-africa-than-blacks-to-us-herland-report/

[cl] https://www.hannenabintuherland.com/usa/white-christian-activist-preachers-and-the-british-empire-abolished-slave-trade/

[cli] https://twitter.com/kingfacef1/status/1270856718487097346?s=21

[clii] https://secure.actblue.com/

[cliii] https://www.hannenabintuherland.com/usa/black-lives-matter-anarchy-riots-will-reelect-law-and-order-trump/

[cliv] https://www.hannenabintuherland.com/usa/george-floyd-not-killed-by-police-autopsy-showed-three-times-fatal-dose-fentanyl-opioid/

[clv] https://www.hannenabintuherland.com/usa/george-floyd-killed-himself-by-drug-overdose-read-medical-examiners-report-police-officer-chauvin-did-not-kill-him/

[clvi] https://www.unz.com/estriker/national-justice-exclusive-brooklyn-based-antifa-network-helping-organize-violence-across-the-country/

[clvii] https://www.wnd.com/2020/06/professionally-led-riots-another-attempted-coup-detat/

[clviii] https://www.hannenabintuherland.com/usa/nancy-pelosi-is-the-rudest-pettiest-lowest-female-in-america-trump-union-address/

[clix] https://letterfromjail.com/

[clx] https://en.wikipedia.org/wiki/From_Dictatorship_to_Democracy

[clxi] https://www.amazon.com/dp/B01FKRZ8ZE/ref=dp-kindle-redirect?_encoding=UTF8&btkr=1

[clxii] https://www.hannenabintuherland.com/europa/snipers-in-maidan-ordered-by-american-instructors-to-shoot-both-policemen-and-demonstrators-newday-news/

[clxiii] https://www.instagram.com/accounts/login/?next=/tv/CA2u_eJDeST/%3Figshid%3D3qi4in0wa26m

[clxiv] https://www.bbc.com/news/world-middle-east-12522848

[clxv] https://www.nytimes.com/2000/11/26/magazine/who-really-brought-down-milosevic.html?pagewanted=6

[clxvi] https://canvasopedia.org/

[clxvii] https://foreignpolicy.com/2011/02/17/revolution-u-2/

[clxviii] https://www.nytimes.com/2000/11/26/magazine/who-really-brought-down-milosevic.html?pagewanted=6

[clxix] https://www.youtube.com/watch?v=lpXbA6yZY-8

[clxx] https://foreignpolicy.com/2011/02/17/revolution-u-2/

[clxxi] https://www.nbcnews.com/politics/donald-trump/mueller-report-conclusions-trump-congress-attorney-general-william-barr-n986611

[clxxii] https://www.washingtonexaminer.com/washington-secrets/rand-paul-investigate-obama-officials-who-concocted-russian-conspiracy-hoax?utm_source=deployer&utm_medium=email&utm_campaign=newslink&utm_term=members&utm_content=20190326191115

[clxxiii] https://www.washingtontimes.com/news/2018/apr/2/over-70-percent-of-americans-see-media-as-fake-new/

[clxxiv] https://www.amazon.com/dp/1949586081

[clxxv] https://www.msn.com/en-us/news/world/syrian-kurds-see-american-betrayal-and-warn-fight-against-isis-is-now-in-doubt/ar-AAIqLHq?ocid=spartanntp

[clxxvi] https://www.nobelprize.org/alfred-nobel/

[clxxvii] https://www.cbsnews.com/news/arafats-billions/

[clxxviii] https://www.vg.no/nyheter/innenriks/i/05Kg0/nobel-slektning-truer-med-aa-frata-norge-fredsprisen [clxxix] https://metro.co.uk/2012/10/12/the-10-controversial-nobel-peace-prize-winners-3816957/

[clxxx] https://rightways.wordpress.com/2010/10/16/politicization-of-nobel-peace-prize/

[clxxxi] https://www.nobelprize.org/alfred-nobel/full-text-of-alfred-nobels-will-2/

[clxxxii] https://www.aftenposten.no/meninger/i/wP6y1/I-strid-med-Nobels-vilje

[clxxxiii] https://www.washingtonpost.com/

[clxxxiv] https://twitter.com/cspan/status/1176194996116086784

[clxxxv] https://www.hannenabintuherland.com/usa/manufacturing-war-with-russia-we-are-in-a-new-and-more-perilous-point-in-a-50-year-nuclear-arms-race/

[clxxxvi] https://www.hannenabintuherland.com/interviews/new-herland-report-show-russia-gate-hoax-was-a-coup-attempt-from-senior-doj-fbi-officials-chris-j-farrell-judicial-watch/

[clxxxvii] https://www.aftenposten.no/verden/i/kyj9/spetakkelet-om-lundestads-nobel-bok-paa-90-sekunder

[clxxxviii] https://www.newsweek.com/greta-thunberg-staring-trump-twitter-1460820

[clxxxix] https://www.hannenabintuherland.com/usa/greta-thunberg-decoy-fossil-free-groups-funded-by-big-oil-billionaires-manipulating/

[cxc] https://www.youtube.com/user/HanneNabintuHerland

[cxci] https://www.harryjacksonministries.com/

[cxcii] https://www.youtube.com/watch?v=JtdaNUu-V2o0&list=PLlrCpcbN8MxjcppbagnHfPKx8Rw-gEHbX4&index=5

[cxciii] https://www.youtube.com/watch?v=lqJ4clx-2Uk0&list=PLlrCpcbN8MxjcppbagnHfPKx8Rw-gEHbX4&index=94

[cxciv] https://www.britannica.com/biography/Martin-Luther-King-Jr

[cxcv] https://www.youtube.com/watch?v=uFmP3YA3i9g

[cxcvi] https://letterfromjail.com/

[cxcvii] https://www.hannenabintuherland.com/in-focus/extremely-dangerous-to-idealize-one-party-in-a-war-soleimani/

[cxcviii] https://www.youtube.com/watch?v=kIM-wvBq1OkU&list=PLlrCpcbN8MxjcppbagnHfPKx8RwgEHbX4&index=5

[cxcix] https://www.nationalreview.com/2020/01/left-mourns-qasem-soleimani/

[cc] https://www.youtube.com/watch?v=xxUbJ-zwl7ZI&list=PLlrCpcbN8MxjcppbagnHfPKx8RwgEHbX4&index=3

[cci] https://twitter.com/rosemcgowan

[ccii] https://twitter.com/rosemcgowan

[cciii] https://www.nationalreview.com/2020/01/left-mourns-qasem-soleimani/

[cciv] https://jcpa.org/article/qasem-soleimani-who-connected-all-the-dots-in-irans-strategy-is-targeted-in-baghdad/

[ccv] https://www.hannenabintuherland.com/europa/jeremy-corbyn-rated-top-anti-semite-2019-infusing-hatred-of-jews-into-west/

[ccvi] https://www.news.com.au/finance/economy/world-economy/bury-them-alive-white-south-africans-fear-for-their-future-as-horrific-farm-attacks-escalate/news-story/3a63389a1b0066b6b0b77522c06d6476

[ccvii] http://www.digitaljournal.com/article/267776

[ccviii] https://www.nzherald.co.nz/business/news/article.cfm?c_id=3&objectid=12003693

[ccix] https://www.politicsweb.co.za/documents/how-the-response-to-black-and-white-racism-differs

[ccx] https://www.theguardian.com/world/2000/jun/03/zimbabwe.andrewmeldrum

[ccxi] https://www.youtube.com/watch?v=lSkpPaiUF8s

[ccxii] https://www.youtube.com/watch?v=hKpMO-5Jdx-s&list=PLlrCpcbN8MxjcppbagnHfPKx8RwgEH-bX4&index=6

[ccxiii] https://www.youtube.com/watch?v=lSkpPaiUF8s

[ccxiv] https://www.dailywire.com/news/covington-catholic-hs-student-nick-sandmann-settles-250-million-lawsuit-with-the-washington-post

[ccxv] https://sports.yahoo.com/nick-sandmann-student-center-viral-162821636.html?guce_referrer=aHR0cHM-6Ly9yLnNlYXJjaC55YWhvby5jb20vX3lsdD1Bd3JD-MUNnNEdTQmZMQThBd1RYUXRETUQ7X3lsd-T1YM29ETVRFeWRuSmpaekE1QkdOdmJHOERZb-Vl4QkhCdmN3TXlCSFowYVdRRFF6QTJOemRmT-VFSelpXTURjM0ktL1JWPTIvUkU9MTU5NTk2Nz-kyOS9STz0xMC9SVT1odHRwcyUzYSUyZiUyZnNwb3J-0cy55YWhvby5jb20lMmZuaWNrLXNhbmRtYW5uLX-N0dWRlbnQtY2VudGVyLXZpcmFsLTE2MjgyM-TYzNi5odG1sL1JLPTIvUlM9Wjh4TDhlUE1maGpk-RURpWE1jSmFCOC5zYkVvLQ&guce_referrer_sig=AQA-AAJaL7aB_rondCfc16oq3oN-ADb_1LbTVl3_CFMQMz-JxV4JxBsdQImNfjx7QSWFMvxBxi4XG6Knr95rh7i4ZklL-3HLkNGjLQZg5kwfOfOQC8PKBhRtjvBeSiQF5mfZXRrg-WGPcjT5oa00PrubpMQd2f2FeaUSsCRos3aQ_n5F_W8g&-guccounter=2

[ccxvi] https://www.hannenabintuherland.com/currentaffairs/the-covington-scandal-defamation-lawsuit-cnn-washing-ton-post-pay-nick-sandmann-500-million-in-damages/

[ccxvii] https://people.com/politics/donald-trump-poses-bible-church-photo-op-after-police-clear-his-path-using-tear-gas/

[ccxviii] https://thefederalist.com/2020/06/01/trump-pays-homage-to-church-burned-in-riots-with-bible-in-hand/

[ccxix] https://christianresearchnetwork.org/2018/04/27/80-of-americans-believe-in-god-pew-found-out-what-they-mean/

[ccxx] https://en.wikipedia.org/wiki/Demographics_of_atheism

[ccxxi] https://www.christianitytoday.com/news/2018/april/we-believe-in-god-what-americans-mean-pew-survey.html

[ccxxii] https://www.amazon.com/History-Modern-World-9th/dp/0375413987

[ccxxiii] https://www.amazon.com/Public-Enemies-Michel-Houellebecq/dp/1848871597

[ccxxiv] https://www.amazon.com/Dialectics-Secularization-Reason-Religion/dp/1586171666

[ccxxv] https://www.amazon.com/Christianity-Crisis-Cultures-Pope-Benedict/dp/1586171429

[ccxxvi] https://letterfromjail.com/

[ccxxvii] https://www.britannica.com/biography/Evagrius-Ponticus

[ccxxviii] https://letterfromjail.com/

[ccxxix] https://letterfromjail.com/

[ccxxx] https://www.wnd.com/2018/12/this-is-why-i-dislike-liberals/

[ccxxxi] https://www.nytimes.com/2018/11/14/technology/facebook-data-russia-election-racism.html

[ccxxxii] https://www.meforum.org/7278/de-platforming-a-new-problem

[ccxxxiii] https://www.theguardian.com/media/2017/aug/06/can-you-trust-mainstream-media

[ccxxxiv] https://thehill.com/homenews/campaign/334897-poll-majority-says-mainstream-media-publishes-fake-news

[ccxxxv] https://www.youtube.com/watch?time_contin-ue=11&v=jdP8TiKY8dE

[ccxxxvi] https://www.activistpost.com/2017/07/cnn-hires-top-al-qaeda-propagandist-documenta-ry-fails-miserably-trying-cover.html

[ccxxxvii] https://www.youtube.com/watch?time_contin-ue=2&v=4dRGMME4VnM

[ccxxxviii] https://www.linkedin.com/pulse/face-book-era-over-gina-bianchini/

[ccxxxix] https://www.youtube.com/watch?v=kc_Jq42Og7Q

[ccxl] https://www.hannenabintuherland.com/englisharticles/facebook-era-is-over-protests-all-over-the-world-too-many-sneaky-controlling-algorithms-jaron-lanier-on-how-social-media-ruins-your-life-herland-report/

[ccxli] https://www.bbc.com/news/technology-44055077

[ccxlii] https://www.theguardian.com/world/2018/may/09/ireland-abortion-referendum-divides-county-roscommon

[ccxliii] https://www.save8.ie/rigged/

[ccxliv] https://www.youtube.com/watch?v=CuS-SgFyjcQ&index=13&list=PLlrCpcbN8MxjcppbagnHfPKx8RwgEHbX4

[ccxlv] https://www.youtube.com/watch?v=U_EM-Wdz5y30&list=PLlrCpcbN8MxjcppbagnHfPKx8RwgEHbX4&index=2

[ccxlvi] https://www.youtube.com/watch?v=ACiWsLmiG-WI&list=PLlrCpcbN8MxjcppbagnHfPKx8RwgEHbX4&index=6

[ccxlvii] https://www.hannenabintuherland.com/usa/the-american-system-is-failing-but-i-think-it-is-good-that-bad-ideas-are-not-successful-dr-ron-paul-to-herland-report-tv/

[ccxlviii] https://www.amazon.com/Origins-Totalitarianism-Hannah-Arendt/dp/0156701537

[ccxlix] https://letterfromjail.com/

CPSIA information can be obtained
at www.ICGtesting.com
Printed in the USA
LVHW081616250920
667123LV00028B/1098

9 781838 127770